David Hölter

Making Leather Knife Sheaths
Volume 3

Welted Sheaths with Snap Fastener and Mexican Loop

4880 Lower Valley Road • Atglen, PA 19310

Copyright © 2016 by Schiffer Publishing, Ltd.

Translated from the German by Ingrid Elser, Dr. John Guess editorial advisor.

Originally published as *Messerscheiden Band 3* by Wieland Verlag, Bad Aibling © 2013 Wieland.

All rights reserved. No part of this work may be reproduced or used in any form or by any means—graphic, electronic, or mechanical, including photocopying or information storage and retrieval systems—without written permission from the publisher.

The scanning, uploading, and distribution of this book or any part thereof via the Internet or any other means without the permission of the publisher is illegal and punishable by law. Please purchase only authorized editions and do not participate in or encourage the electronic piracy of copyrighted materials.

"Schiffer," "Schiffer Publishing, Ltd.," and the pen and inkwell logo are registered trademarks of Schiffer Publishing, Ltd.

Library of Congress Control Number: 2011944425

Photos: Peter Fronteddu (pages 66–67, 144–149),
Hans Joachim Wieland (all other photos)
Type set in Courier, Frutiger and Times

ISBN: 978-0-7643-5022-1
Printed in China

Published by Schiffer Publishing, Ltd.
4880 Lower Valley Road
Atglen, PA 19310
Phone: (610) 593-1777; Fax: (610) 593-2002
E-mail: Info@schifferbooks.com
Web: www.schifferbooks.com

CONTENTS

A Few Words Up Front 4
Preface 6
Introduction 7

1. **Project I: Mexican Loop Sheath 8**
   1.1 Planning and Design of the Sheath 8
   1.2 Creating the Template 11
   1.3 Preparing the Parts for Construction 30
      1.3.1 Preparing the Front Blade with Embossing . 31
      1.3.2 Fitting the Welt 39
      1.3.3 Gluing and Cleaning the Sheath Body 43
      1.3.4 Fitting the Mexican Loop 45
   1.4 Sewing the Sheath 64
   1.5 Attaching the Protective Strap 75
   1.6 Dyeing the Sheath 83
   1.7 Sealing the Cut Edges
         and Impregnating the Leather 86

2. **Project II: Welted Sheath with Snap Fastener 90**
   2.1 Planning and Design of the Sheath 90
   2.2 Creating the Template 93
   2.3 Preparing the Parts for Construction 102
      2.3.1 Making the Sheath's Back Blade 104
      2.3.2 Making the Sheath's Front Blade 111
      2.3.3 Fitting the Welt 117
   2.4 Gluing and Sewing the Sheath 119
   2.5 Cleaning the Cut Edges 125
   2.6 Making the Flap 129
   2.7 Sealing the Cut Edges
         and Impregnating the Leather 137
   Basics 142
   Choice of Materials 142
   The Tools 147
   Glossary 150

A FEW WORDS UP FRONT

Knifemaking as a hobby has created a wide circle of friends. Many people have discovered how much joy it can be to make such a pretty yet practical device on their own. And of course, a pretty knife needs a quality sheath—at least with fixed blades. In addition, many knives manufactured in series only come with rather simple sheaths. A high-quality, handmade sheath can increase the value of any knife.

Working with leather brings a lot of pleasure and is not very demanding with respect to the equipment in your workshop. Special knowledge is not a prerequisite, either. Anyone who is a bit skilled can make a leather sheath on their own. What you have to know you will learn here. All the rest is practice, practice, practice.

This volume complements the topic of knife sheaths that started with Volume 1 and was continued in Volume 2. We once again introduce two different sheath models with different designs and technical solutions. These are so-called welted or welt-sewn sheaths.

At the end of this book you will find the most important basics regarding materials and tools. This way you can enter the series with this volume without having read the other volumes first.

A Few Words Up Front

This workshop series wants to help you with all technical questions and spare you quite a few errors. This series of books assembles a multitude of themes all around knifemaking, enabling you not only to follow each step, but to do it yourself, too. We emphasize the usability of all the volumes in workshop practice.

Thus, all the volumes are provided with a wire binding; this way the book stays open when you put it down. Also, we took care that the size of images and fonts is big enough to still be recognizable and readable when the book is lying next to you during work.

We have tried to explain every work step in the most comprehensive way, but before you pick up your tools, you nevertheless ought to completely read all the descriptions and explanations in this book. This way, you will know what to expect and will not be confronted with unpleasant surprises later on. By means of the materials and tools lists you can put together what you need in advance.

And now I wish you much fun and success with your work!

Hans Joachim Wieland
Chief Editor, MESSER MAGAZIN

PREFACE

In today's service-oriented society, craftsmanship increasingly falls into oblivion. Quite often the quality of the craftsmanship and the longevity of products are no longer of importance. Hence, it is no wonder that more and more crafts enterprises and workshops have vanished from the streets of our cities in the course of the last few decades.

It is all the more a joy to note that increasingly more people are re-thinking and searching for a path leading away from mass products. In the process, they invest time and patience learning more about ancient crafts and forgotten techniques, and some turn the acquired knowledge into works of their own.

This book continues with the welt-sewn leather sheaths that started with *Making Leather Knife Sheaths Volume 2*. We developed two very interesting and quite unusual projects to show the multitude of construction types and technical possibilities.

This volume can be used as a stand-alone work or as a supplement to the already published volumes. For beginners we added the basics about materials and tools in the appendix. The most important technical expressions are explained in a glossary as well.

I wish you much pleasure in reading and hope that we can give you a few ideas and tips for your next projects. A very special thanks to Hans Joachim Wieland, who this time was not only acting behind the scenes, but also showcased the marvelous photos accompanying this volume.

David Hölter

INTRODUCTION

For the design and construction of a leather sheath for a fixed blade there are various possibilities. Depending on the type of knife, several given facts have to be taken into account to make the leather sheath in the optimal way. In this book we will describe in depth the making of two welted leather sheaths, their design features, and the ways of producing them. We will introduce different variants to show a system with which a proper leather sheath can be made for common as well as fancy blade shapes.

During the production, we will show the execution of each work step mainly manually, because no machine can reproduce the delicate finesse necessary for processing leather. We show how to use the tools for processing leather, as well as the basics of working with this material. The actual realization nevertheless is up to each sheathmaker. Thus, we see this book less as a manual for specific leather sheaths and more as a means of providing our readers with the basis for the realization of their own ideas.

Knife sheaths are more than just a means for transporting knives and storing them. Quite often they are individual pieces of art, tailored to the person carrying the knife, their knife, and its needs. In this book we can only mention the basics, since the unlimited possibilities for personalization are far beyond the scope of this volume. We nevertheless invite you to set your own creativity free and implement your own ideas without restraint. The basic requirement for a knife sheath is the safe and reliable accommodation of the knife. It has to protect the person carrying the knife from inadvertent injury from the sharp edge while at the same time protect the knife from external influences. This entails some important aspects that have to be taken into account with design and construction.

PROJECT I:
Mexican Loop Sheath

1.1 Planning and Design of the Sheath

For this somewhat complex project we chose a Bowie knife for which we will construct a so-called Mexican loop sheath. The Mexican loop sheath consists of a welt-sewn sheath body that will hold the knife blade and an added loop acting as a belt loop.

The specialty of this construction is the main loop. The lower part of the sheath body is threaded into this loop by means of a smaller loop. This way the width of the belt loop can be adjusted. If needed, the sheath body can be removed and the sheath taken off the belt without having to detach the belt from the trousers first.

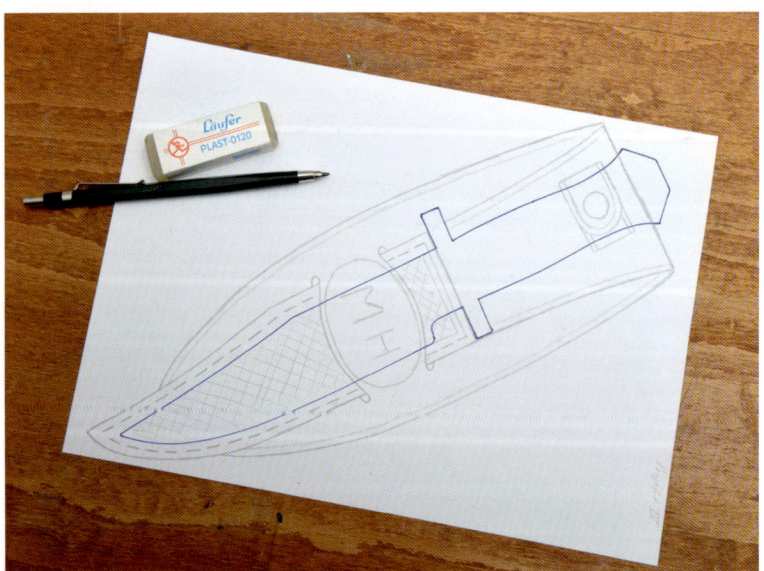

The basis for working is a design drawing. We first transfer the contour of the knife, then decide on the contour of the sheath and draw all the details.

1.1 Planning and Design of the Sheath

The sheath body is to receive an embossing with a basketweave pattern. We also want to punch the initials of the owner into the smaller loop integrated into the larger Mexican loop. We will dye the sheath a dark reddish brown fitting to the cocobolo handle of the knife.

Our construction will be made for a left-handed person. If you plan your project for a right-handed person, you simply work mirrored compared to this manual. We start with the design and make a draft into which we draw the details.

MATERIALS AND TOOLS

Materials
- thick drawing paper
- 2 harness needles, size 2
- DIN A3/ledger size
- 1 adjustable groover
- tape
- 1 edge beveler, size 3
- smooth, full-grain leather
- 1 edge beveler, size 4
- thickness 3.5 – 4.0 mm
- 1 wing dividers
- kid leather, thickness 0.2 – 0.5 mm
- 1 drive punch, 4 mm
- plastic sinew
- 1 drive punch, 5 mm
- contact adhesive
- 1 V gouge
- leather dye based on spirit
- 1 scratch awl, width about 3 mm
- color tan
- 1 handle for scratch awl
- antique finish, color brown
- 1 base for piercing
- transparent edge sealant
- 2 sponges
- plastic wrap
- 1 cigarette lighter
- leather grease with beeswax
- 1 embossing stamp, shell pattern
- 1 embossing stamp

Tools
- 1 pencil
- 1 small circular stamp
- 1 eraser
- 1 set of letter stamps
- 1 geometrical set square or
- 1 set of ornamental stamps
- protractor
- 1 stone base
- 1 curve template
- 1 mallet
  (rawhide, wood or plastics)
- 1 caliper
- 1 shoemaker's hammer
  (with polished steel surfaces)
- 1 tape measure
- 1 paper scissors
- 1 pliers with smooth jaws
- 1 cutting board (plastic or wood)
- 2 paint brushes, width 10 – 20 mm
- 1 shoemaker's knife
- 4 pairs of disposable gloves
- 1 bone folder or handmade
- 1 shoe brush
- horn tool
- 1 piece of cotton cloth
- 1 modeling tool

Project 1: Mexican Loop Sheath

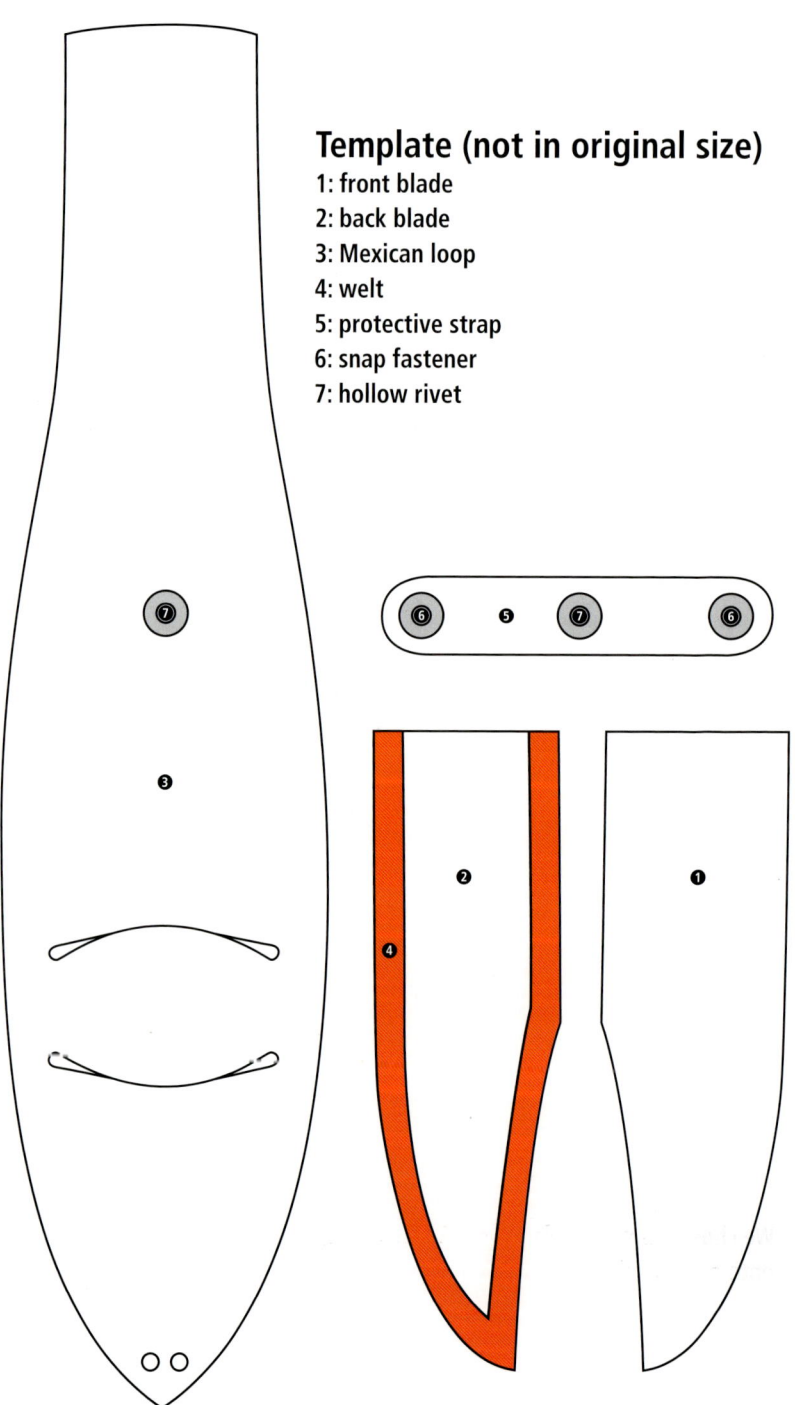

1.2 Creating the Template

First we prepare our drawing place. We start by creating the template for our Mexican loop sheath. For this we draw the outline of the Bowie knife on a piece of thick drawing paper. The sheath body will be dealt with first.

We draw the end of the guard towards the blade into our drawing of the outlines. Later, the sheath will rest against it. Since the blade's shape is rectangular in the rear part, we draw parallel lines at a distance of about ⁵⁄₁₆" (eight millimeters) to the edge and back of the knife blade. We continue these lines at a distance of ⁵⁄₁₆" (8 mm)—following the blade's shape—until they cross each other at the tip. This way we achieve the basic shape of our later sheath body.

We chose a Bowie knife for our Mexican loop sheath. We put the knife onto a piece of thick drawing paper and follow its contour with a pencil.

Project 1: Mexican Loop Sheath

We draw the upper end of the sheath in our sketch with the geometrical set square. Later it will rest against the knife's guard.

We draw the contour of our planned sheath. Here you have to take into account that the welt needs about 5/16" (eight millimeters) of space.

1.2 Creating the Template

We draw the contour of the sheath's tip on our design drawing.

The seam and decorative lines are drawn with the pencil. In the center of the sheath's front blade we leave an area for the later embossing.

Project 1: Mexican Loop Sheath

Now the later course of the seam is drawn in. The seam will run at a distance of about ³⁄₁₆" (four to five millimeters) to the sheath's outside. At the sheath orifice we draw a decorative line ³⁄₁₆" (four millimeters) towards the rim. To create the area for the later basketweave embossing we follow the outline of the knife blade. This means we only have to draw a second line in the upper area of the sheath at a distance of about ⁵⁄₁₆" (eight millimeters) towards the rim.

The template is cut out with scissors. For the further design and creating other templates we transfer the outline of the sheath body onto thick drawing paper and draw the contour of the knife handle.

The Mexican loop should reach almost up to the knife handle's end. Thus, by means of the geometric set square, we draw a parallel to the upper end of the sheath body at a distance of about ³⁄₈" (1 cm below the handle's end.

The template for the sheath's front blade is cut out with scissors.

1.2 Creating the Template

We transfer the contour of the sheath's front blade onto the thick drawing paper and draw the knife handle.

The upper end of the belt loop is drawn parallel to the upper end of the sheath using a pencil and a geometrical set square.

Project 1: Mexican Loop Sheath

Using a geometrical set square we draw a line parallel to the sheath's upper end. We place this line centered in the upper half of the sheath body.

We draw the sheath's center line and extend it beyond the handle's end. Parallel to the sheath's upper end we draw the conclusion of the later belt loop at about the same place the pommel is located.

1.2 Creating the Template

Next we determine the central point of the later small loop. It ought to be placed centered on the upper half of the sheath body. We draw the center line of the sheath body. The central point of the later small loop lies at the intersection of both lines.

Then we draw the course of the Mexican loop between the upper end of the sheath body and the upper end of the loop. Since the loop ought to be symmetrical later on, we first draw one side only and then mirror it. Our sheath body is about 2 ⅜" (six centimeters) wide. For the Mexican loop we need approximately 1 3⁄16" (two additional centimeters) to the left and right, meaning the loop will later be about 3 15⁄16" (ten centimeters) wide at its broadest point.

The transition between the upper end of the sheath body and the loop's upper end is designed as a flowing line. Thus, we add ⅜" (one centimeter) to the right and left at the upper end. This means we draw about 1 9⁄16" (four centimeters) at the upper end of the Mexican loop.

We use the curve template to draw the contour of the belt loop.

Project 1: Mexican Loop Sheath

Now we mark the position of the Mexican loop. For this we set a mark about 1³⁄₁₆" (20 millimeters) from the sheath's rim. Later this will be the broadest area of the Mexican loop.

Now we draw the outline of the Mexican loop using the curve template. We start at our mark and draw towards the sheath's tip.

1.2 Creating the Template

Then we continue the line to the upper end of the belt loop. Now we have finished drawing the outline of half the Mexican loop.

Now you connect the upper end of the sheath body and the upper end of the loop with a fine sweep. For this we use the curve template. Next we mark the broadest point of the Mexican loop—which lies at the position of the later small loop—and also mark our add-on of about $1\frac{3}{16}$" (two centimeters). Using the curve template, we continue the sweep from the upper end of the Mexican loop down towards the sheath's tip. The loop will end about $1\frac{3}{16}$" (two centimeters) prior to reaching the blade tip, but there are no limits with respect to design.

Now we start drawing the course and shape of the small loop. For this, we first set two marks about $\frac{3}{16}$" (five millimeters) away from the sheath body and each $1\frac{1}{16}$" (18 millimeters) to the center line of the small loop. The loop is supposed to later have an oval shape and contain a monogram embossing framed by an oval. For this we set marks on the center line of the sheath body at 1" (25 millimeters) each to the loop's center line. The marked points are connected with a suitable sweep by means of the curve template.

Project 1: Mexican Loop Sheath

On our design drawing we now mark the spots where the small loop will be cut out later.

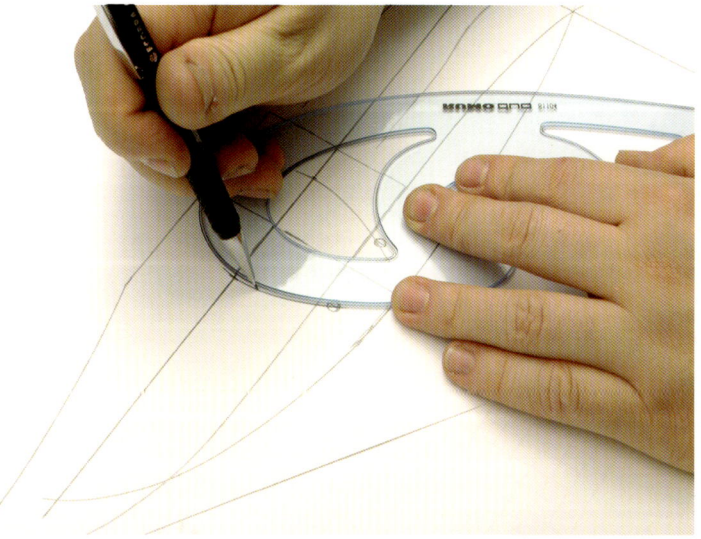

Since we want to add a monogram later and want to make the small loop look somewhat prettier, the small loop is designed as an oval. For this we take our curve template and draw a quarter of the oval each at the top and bottom of the small loop.

1.2 Creating the Template

Now we have the sketch of half the Mexican loop in front of us. We fold the drawing paper along the drawing's center line. To create a sharp fold we press the fold flat with the bone folder. Then we cut out the contour of the Mexican loop. While the drawing paper is still folded, we punch the marked points for the small loop with the ³⁄₁₆" (4 millimeter) drive punch.

To transfer the course of the small loop onto our final template, we cut out the drawn outline with the shoemaker's knife. The template is unfolded and we now have the first part of the Mexican loop before us. To check its shape we push the template of the sheath body through the small loop.

The transition of the Mexican loop connecting it to the sheath body is still missing. Thus, we transfer the outline of the loop's template onto thick drawing paper. Our marked points for the small loop and the outline of the small loop are transferred through the slits in the drawing paper as well.

The contour of our sheath as well as half of the Mexican loop in overview.

Project 1: Mexican Loop Sheath

The sketch is folded along its center line.

With the bone folder we tighten the fold to get a template that is as accurate as possible.

1.2 Creating the Template

The scissors in action: the outline of the template is cut out.

With the drive punch we set the points for the later transition of the small loop from our template.

Project 1: Mexican Loop Sheath

With the shoemaker's knife we cut the contour of the small loop along our mark.

The sheath will be put through this small loop to fix it to the belt.

To check the design, we put the previously made sheath template through the loop. Here you can see that there is still some play to the left and right. The later sheath will be a good deal thicker. It consists of the front and back blades as well as the welt.

We draw the contour of our created template onto a big piece of thick drawing paper.

1.2 Creating the Template

The contours of our later small loop are transferred as well.

Now the slits of the small loop on our template are closed by taping them shut from the backside. The template is folded along the center line and cut apart at the center line of the small loop. Then we cut out the contour of the Mexican loop along the sheath body to the upper end.

The template is joined to the upper end of the drawing and its contours are transferred. Now we see the complete outline of the Mexican loop.

We still need a template for the welt. For this we first copy the outline of the sheath body's template. Then we cut the welt's template by following the contour of the knife blade on our drawing.

The templates for the Mexican loop and the sheath body are cut from the drawing paper as well. Now we have prepared all the templates we need for making the sheath.

Project 1: Mexican Loop Sheath

We tape the cutouts for the loop from the backside.

With scissors we cut along the previously drawn centerline of the loop on our template.

1.2 Creating the Template

Now we use the scissors to cut the outline of the belt loop's front side that we designed first.

We put the template onto our sketch at the later folding point of the belt loop and transfer the contour.

Project 1: Mexican Loop Sheath

Now our template for the Mexican loop is finished.

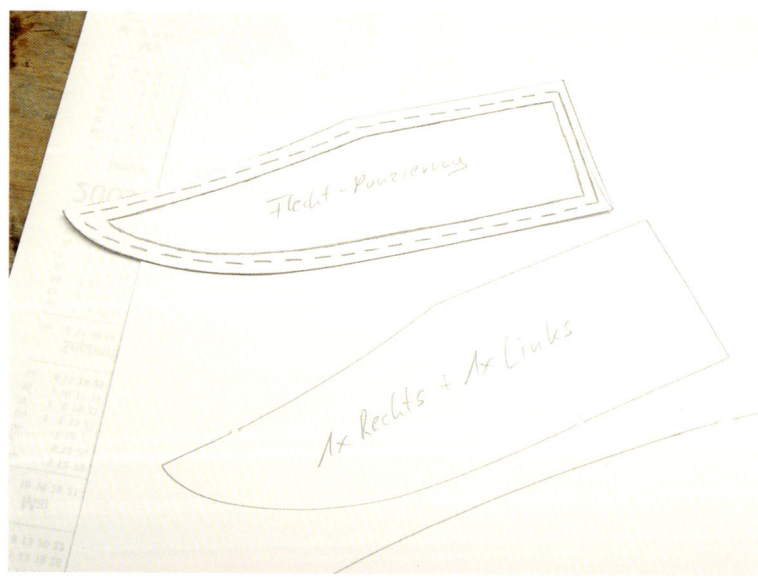

To make a fitting welt from our sheath template, we once again draw the already existing template onto thick drawing paper. We will need it later for the sheath's front and back blades.

1.2 Creating the Template

The pattern for the later welt is now cut from the template.

The other templates are cut from the drawing paper as well. Now we have all the templates we need for our Mexican loop sheath.

1.3 Preparing the Parts for Construction

For our sheath we choose robust and smooth full-grain leather with a thickness of about 3.5 to 4.0 millimeters. When drawing the construction parts we have to take the leather's direction of pull into account. It is especially important for the Mexican loop and has to be chosen in a way that the leather can't be pulled along the loop's longitudinal axis. If the loop is cut out in the leather's direction of pull the loop may become longer over time.

For better visibility we drew the contours with a black felt pen, but we recommend working with a pencil to avoid unwanted color stripes on the sheath.

We need a separate part for the front blade of the sheath body as well as for its back blade. For this, we draw the outline of the front blade once more but mirrored. Afterwards, we cut out the individual parts with a shoemaker's knife. You ought to use a cutting board while doing so.

Now we draw the templates onto the leather. To hold the big bowie knife we chose smooth, full-grain leather with a thickness of about 3.5–4.0 mm. Afterwards, the parts are cut out with a shoemaker's knife.

1.3 Preparing the Parts for Construction

1.3.1 Preparing the Front Blade with Embossing

We start making the sheath's front blade. For this, we take the prepared cut-out leather and the welt's template. With the adjustable groover—set to a width of about ⁵⁄₁₆" (eight millimeters)—we cut a decorative groove along the rim into the upper surface of the leather. Later it will become the boundary of our embossing.

The sheath's front blade is prepared by taking the template at hand and setting the adjustable groover to the width of the welt.

Project 1: Mexican Loop Sheath

With the adjustable groover prepared we draw a groove on the leather's outside along the rim.

We set the adjustable groover to half the previously drawn groove distance and draw a second groove parallel to the first one. Here we will sew our seam later on.

1.3 Preparing the Parts for Construction

Thereafter, the adjustable groover is set to a distance of about ³⁄₁₆" (five millimeters) and a second groove is drawn. This will be used later on for the seam. We decided to emboss the front side of our sheath with a basketweave pattern. For this we chose a suitable embossing stamp, as well as one with a shell pattern that we will use later for the transition towards our limiting groove.

The leather surface is prepared by moistening it evenly with a wet sponge. To align the embossing by means of the horn tool we draw an auxiliary line onto the leather at a 45° angle to the sheath's center line. Now we place the punches next to each other using the auxiliary line for guidance.

We decided on a basketweave pattern for embossing the sheath's front side. For this, we decided on an embossing stamp for embossing the whole area and on another one that we will use to decorate the margins.

We moisten the leather surface with a sponge. Take care to apply the water evenly.

Project 1: Mexican Loop Sheath

We use the geometrical set square to draw an auxiliary line along which we will align our embossing. For this we choose an angle of about 45° and slightly press the auxiliary line into the leather surface using the horn tool.

We align our embossing stamp with the auxiliary line and punch it into the leather with a mallet. Now we can align the embossing stamp with the patterns already punched into the leather.

When punching the stamps into the leather, you have to take care to always punch vertically to create a clear imprint and a uniform pattern.

1.3 Preparing the Parts for Construction

We use a stone base for our work and punch the embossing pattern into the moist leather using a rawhide mallet. If no rawhide mallet is at hand, you can also use a plastic or wooden mallet. We work overlapping when applying the basketweave pattern, which results in a very uniform pattern.

We emboss the entire inside area. While doing so, we have to take care not to cross the limiting groove. You can also tilt the embossing stamp slightly to avoid crossing the groove, but you have to work very carefully. Embossing large areas is easiest if you start at the auxiliary line: first you work on one half and then the other.

Close to the rim it can be helpful to hold the embossing stamp slightly tilted to prevent the pattern from crossing the groove cut previously. Here you have to use a mallet very carefully to avoid imprinting the pattern too deeply because of the stamp's smaller contact area.

Project 1: Mexican Loop Sheath

We place the punches next to each other and decorate the sheath with a uniform pattern.

It is helpful to moisten the leather every once in a while to treat it smoothly and uniformly.

Now we work on the margins of the embossed area. Here we use the stamp with a shell pattern starting in the corners.

1.3 Preparing the Parts for Construction

We put a small circular punch directly in the corner.

We put the shell embossing evenly spaced along the groove.

With a modeling tool we work on the groove in such a way as to round it towards the embossing.

Now our self-made horn tool comes into use. We prepared it for the task of rounding the grooves.

In case the leather gets too dry during work simply moisten the leather surface again with the sponge. We also moisten the leather after applying the basketweave pattern. We start by punching the shell pattern in the three corners. Optionally, you can also set an additional, small circular embossing into the corners. Now we connect the corner points along the limiting line by setting shell next to shell, creating an elegant framing effect.

The edges are carefully refined with the sharpened tip of our tool.

Embossing the front side of our sheath is finished.

1.3 Preparing the Parts for Construction

To create a prettier transition toward the grooves we round the groove towards the embossing slightly using our modeling tool. Afterwards, we use our self-made horn tool to round the space between both grooves. The corners are reworked with the tip of our horn tool. Then our front blade is ready for further work.

1.3.2 Fitting the Welt

To make the welt, we first measure the thickness of the knife blade. Our blade measures 3/16" (five millimeters) at its back close to the guard, tapering towards the tip to a thickness of less than 1/16" (1 millimeter). Since we already cut the welt from leather 3.5 millimeters thick we have to strengthen it a bit. For this we put the knife blade inside the

To prepare the welt, we first measure the knife blade's thickness.

Since the knife blade is about 3/16" (five millimeters) thick and tapers towards the tip we have to strengthen the welt we already cut from smooth, full-grain leather with a thickness of 3.5–4.0 mm.

Project 1: Mexican Loop Sheath

welt and mark its increasing thickness on the welt. We take smooth, full-grain leather with a 1.5-millimeter thickness from our box of scraps and leftovers. For this type of work, leather pieces left over from previous work or from cutting pieces to size are well suited. If the leather is too thick it can be thinned to the right thickness with a shoemaker's knife or ground on a belt grinder.

Both leather strips are glued on using contact adhesive, then the transition towards the blade tip is skived according to the knife blade's thickness. While doing so, we do not skive the leather towards the blade tip but keep the 3.5-millimeter thickness.

Now we take the front and back blades of the sheath, put the knife blade on them, and draw its outline onto the flesh side of the leather. The prepared welt is then glued with contact adhesive onto the flesh side of the sheath's front blade. Fitting and alignment of the welt are checked once more by inserting the knife blade. The blade should fit closely to the welt without play. If the welt shows too much strain it has to be reworked.

To strengthen the welt we glue pieces of smooth, full-grain leather onto the parts that need strengthening and skive the transitions towards the blade tip with the shoemaker's knife.

1.3 Preparing the Parts for Construction

Now we transfer the outline of the knife blade onto the backside of the sheath's front blade, as well as the backside of the sheath's back blade.

An overview of our prepared construction parts.

Project 1: Mexican Loop Sheath

With contact adhesive we glue the welt along the marked contour lines onto the sheath's front blade.

We once again check the fit of the knife blade.

1.3.3 Gluing and Cleaning the Sheath Body

Now we cover the welt and the flesh side of the sheath's back blade with contact adhesive and place them together after setting. When the construction parts are lying on top of each other congruently we press them together with our fingers and additionally pat them together on a firm base using a shoemaker's hammer.

The outer edge of the sheath is ground flush with a belt grinder. Here you should take care to always use fresh, sharp grinding belts and a slow grinding speed. The cut edges of the entire sheath are broken with the edge beveler size 4. The sheath orifice is cleaned by means of the edge beveler size 3. At places that are hard to reach we refine them freehand with the shoemaker's knife to break all edges and prevent coarse leather fibers from sticking out. Afterwards, the cut edges are moistened evenly with the sponge. With our horn tool we round the cut edges, smooth them, and bring them to a shine.

The welt and the sheath's back blade are covered with contact adhesive along the markings.

Afterwards, the construction parts of the sheath body are glued together fittingly.

Project 1: Mexican Loop Sheath

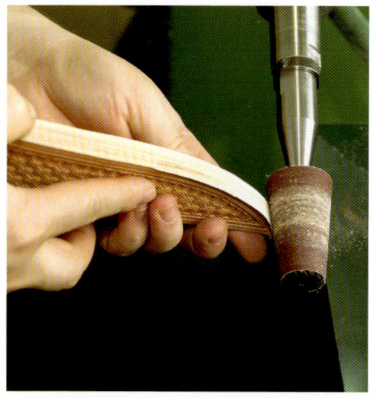 

Using a grinding machine we grind the welt flush with the other construction parts of the sheath.

The edges are broken evenly using the edge beveler size 4.

Using a sponge we evenly moisten the freshly ground cut edges.

We smooth the edges with our horn tool until they shine and round them evenly.

1.3 Preparing the Parts for Construction

1.3.4 Fitting the Mexican Loop

During the next work step we want to fit the Mexican loop. For this we turn the cut-out leather so that the flesh side is up. Then we take our template and mark the upper side of the sheath body on the leather.

We start transferring the line where the loop overlaps with the sheath from the template to the flesh side of the Mexican loop.

With the shoemaker's knife we skive the transition cleanly down to a leather thickness of about 1/16" (one millimeter).

Project 1: Mexican Loop Sheath

The area where the Mexican loop will be connected with the sheath body later is skived with the shoemaker's knife to a thickness of about 1/16" (one millimeter) so there will not be an abrupt transition between the individual construction parts later on.

The Mexican loop is turned onto its grain side and we draw a groove at a distance of about 3/16" (four millimeters) to the rim using an adjustable groover.

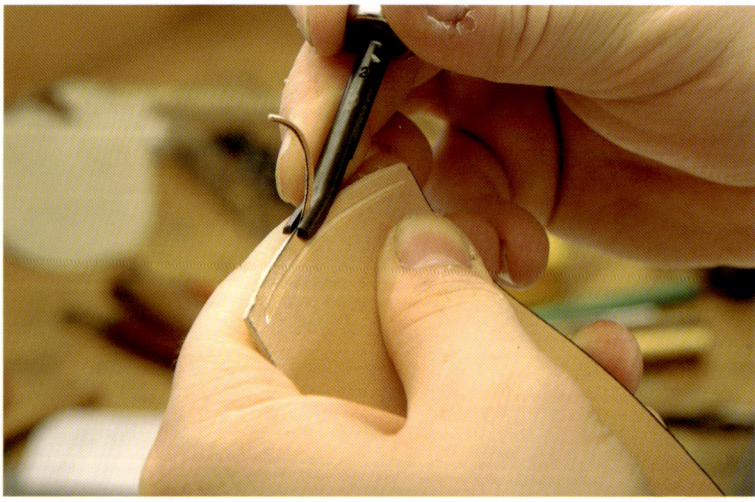

With the edge beveler size 2 we break the edge on the grain side of the leather.

1.3 Preparing the Parts for Construction

With the edge beveler size 2 we break the edge on the grain side of the leather.

The edge is moistened and smoothed with the horn tool.

The bulge created on the flesh side is carefully removed with the shoemaker's knife.

Project 1: Mexican Loop Sheath

After skiving, we turn the loop around and draw a decorative groove about ³⁄₁₆" (four millimeters) to the loop's skived end. The cut edge is broken with the edge beveler size 2 and moistened evenly. With our horn tool we round the edge uniformly and bring it to a shine. The resulting bulge that is created on the flesh side is carefully removed with the shoemaker's knife.

Now we come to the most difficult part: adjusting the small loop that will hold the sheath body. For this we take the already prepared sheath body and measure its circumference at the point the loop will be later located. Our sheath body has a circumference of 5⁵⁄₁₆" (13.5 centimeters) at this place.

To adjust the small loop that will later hold the sheath we first measure the circumference of the already prepared sheath.

The measured circumference of 5⁵⁄₁₆" (13.5 cm) is divided by two and a small surplus is added for the sheath to be threaded in and removed easier later on. The determined measurement is drawn symmetrically onto the prepared template at the place where the small loop is supposed to be later on.

1.3 Preparing the Parts for Construction

We take the template of the Mexican loop and calculate the width of the smaller loop by dividing the circumference of the sheath by two, adding 1/16" to 1/8" (two to three millimeters) to ease pushing in and drawing the sheath later on. The calculated 2¾" (seven centimeters) for the small loop is drawn centered onto the template.

Our preliminary marks we drew while making the template are consistent with our calculated measurements. This is not always the case, because the blade's thickness and thus the required thickness of the welt and the thickness of the used leather for the sheath's front and back blades can differ from project to project, so this step should in no case be omitted.

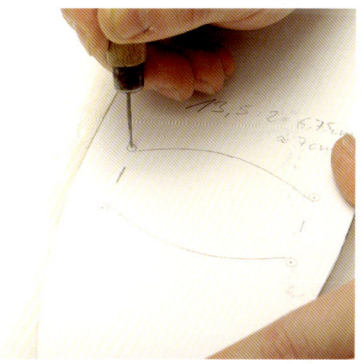

With the scratch awl we pierce the corner points of the small loop.

The oval contour of the loop is cut out with the shoemaker's knife.

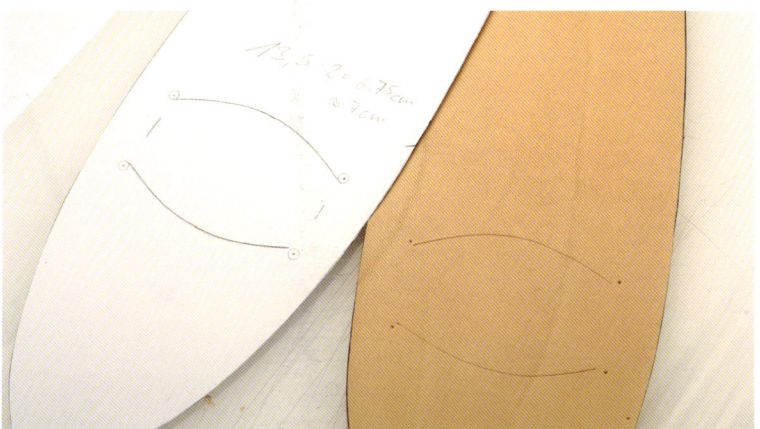

The template is put onto our prepared Mexican loop and the corner points and the contour are marked.

Project 1: Mexican Loop Sheath

The calculated width of the small loop is marked at the four corners and punched through the template using the awl. Afterwards, the upper and lower contours of the loop are cut out with the shoemaker's knife. The template is put onto the upper surface of the leather and the upper and lower contours and the four corner points are transferred.

With the ³⁄₁₆" (5 millimeter) drive punch we punch out the drawn corner points.

Now we cut the oval loop with the shoemaker's knife.

1.3 Preparing the Parts for Construction

We punch the corner holes with the ³⁄₁₆" (5 millimeter) drive punch. The contours of the small loop are cut out carefully with the shoemaker's knife. Here we start at the corner holes, cut until a bit beyond the center, then cut the rest starting at the opposite corner hole. This way you avoid inadvertently cutting into the area close to the rim.

At the previously punched corner points we cut out a small wedge.

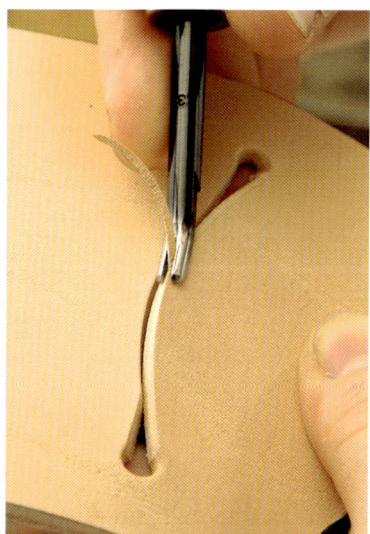

The thus created cut edges are broken with the edge beveler size 3.

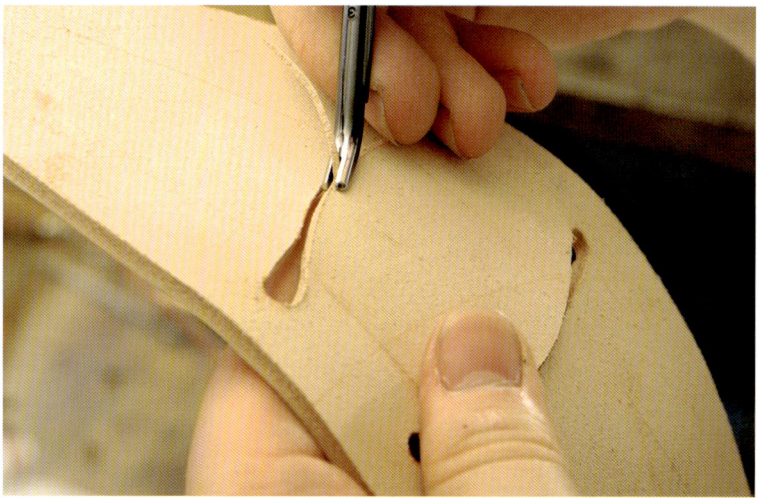

The cut edges on the backside of the Mexican loop are also broken cleanly.

Project 1: Mexican Loop Sheath

When cutting the small loop, you absolutely have to take care cutting. The cutting always has to be vertical, at a 90° angle toward the leather surface. At each of the punched corner holes you cut a small wedge from the leather, enhancing the look. Afterwards, the cut edges on the front and back are broken with the edge beveler size 3.

Now we come to the oval decoration on the center of the small loop. We will later emboss the center of this oval with the monogram. For this, we cut out the small loop of the template by connecting the four corner holes. We put our curve template to one of the four corner points and draw a fine sweep, continuing the contour of the loop and leading to the center of the small loop at the outside edge of the template.

We fold the loop template centered, then once more to achieve quarters. This way we are able to create a symmetrical template for the oval. To this end, we first cut the drawn sweep off all four corners at the same time. Since the frame around the monogram should be a bit smaller than the loop, we reduce the size by ³⁄₁₆" (four millimeters) by drawing a uniform border of ³⁄₁₆" (four millimeters) and cutting the template to size with scissors.

We take the paper template at hand and cut out the small loop.

1.3 Preparing the Parts for Construction

To create a perfect oval later on we draw the transitions at the right and left sides onto the template.

The template is folded along its longitudinal axis.

Thereafter it is folded once more crosswise.

Project 1: Mexican Loop Sheath

Now we cut out our template with the scissors.

We draw a line at about 3/16" (four millimeters) to the rim.

Then we cut our template to size with the scissors.

1.3 Preparing the Parts for Construction

We unfold the created template and place it centered on the front side of our small leather loop. Here the folding lines prove very useful for correct positioning. We transfer the outline of our template onto the leather surface with a pencil.

Now it gets really difficult; the next work step requires a lot of fine motor skills and sharp tools. With the V gouge we cut a uniform groove into the leather following the mark. To do so, you should practice with scrap leather, because you can't afford any slip on the leather with the V gouge. For the monogram we have procured western-style letter stamps. These can be obtained from specialized dealers as complete alphabets in different fonts and letter sizes.

This way we create a perfect oval that we place centered on our small loop and transfer onto the leather with a pencil.

With a V gouge we cut the groove into the leather along the drawn oval.

The area on which the monogram should be punched is moistened evenly with a sponge. The letter stamps come along with an attachable handle, easing the placement of the stamps. Now we press one stamp after another into the moist leather by giving them a hard, vertical punch with the rawhide mallet. As we did for embossing the sheath's front blade, we use a stone base for this work step.

We want to embellish our Mexican loop sheath with a monogram. For this we use letter stamps in Western style.

The place to be punched is moistened with water.

Because the embossing stamps have a removable handle they can be centered and aligned before punching them into the moist leather.

Then we punch the embossing stamps with a rawhide mallet.

1.3 Preparing the Parts for Construction

Both of our letters have been imprinted cleanly and evenly into the moist leather. To round off the visual impression we put two ornamental punches above and below each of the letters. Finished!

The initials are cleanly impressed into the leather's surface.

For embellishment we chose two nicely curved ornaments that we also punch into the leather.

Project 1: Mexican Loop Sheath

For the surrounding, decorative groove of the Mexican loop we set the adjustable groover to the same distance we used for the seam distance on the sheath body. The decorative groove is cut into the leather on its grain as well as its flesh side. Afterward, all the cut edges are broken with the edge beveler (size 3).

We set the adjustable groover to the same distance we used for the seam distance on the sheath.

Now we draw a decorative groove along the outside edge.

We also draw a groove on the backside of the Mexican loop.

1.3 Preparing the Parts for Construction

We check the later position of the loop.

With the edge beveler size 3 we break the outside edges of the Mexican loop on the front and the backside.

At the tip of the Mexican loop we punch two adjacent holes into the leather by means of the 3/16" (5 millimeter) drive punch. Here we later thread in the lace for attaching the sheath to the thigh. We start by cleaning the loop: first we moisten the cut edges of the small loop, then we round and smooth them with the horn tool until they shine. Afterward, we treat the outer cut edges of the entire Mexican loop the same way, but use a so-called burnishing wheel for the long cut edges. The burnishing wheel works similarly to our horn tool.

Project 1: Mexican Loop Sheath

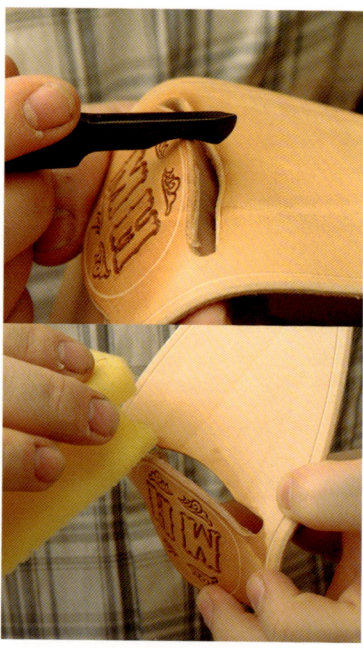

At the lower tapering end of the loop we punch two symmetrical holes into the leather. The thigh lace will be fastened at these holes later on.

Now we start cleaning the edges. We smooth all cut edges by first moistening them, then making them shine with our horn tool.

For the long outsides of the loop we use the burnishing wheel.

1.3 Preparing the Parts for Construction

Our Mexican loop is almost finished. We now put the sheath body into the small loop, fold the belt loop backwards, and push it downwards underneath the sheath body until it reaches the mark. Now the small loop is slipped to its intended place on the sheath body. This way we gain the exact folding point of the Mexican loop that will form the belt loop. We thoroughly moisten the loop in the area where it is folded until the leather can be easily shaped and then press the fold flat with our fingers.

The fit of the individual components is checked.

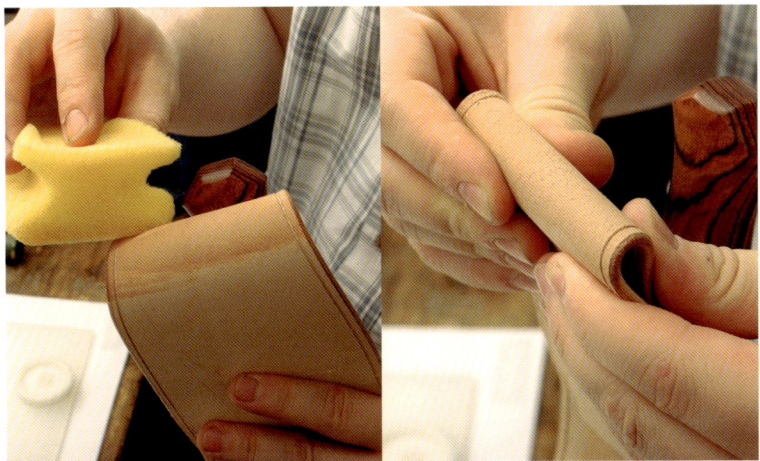

The loop is moistened on the top surface and pressed together.

Project 1: Mexican Loop Sheath

Now both parts are ready for gluing. We pull the sheath body from the small loop and place the Mexican loop at its later location. On the backside of the sheath body we draw the overlapping end of the loop with the pencil. The leather surface is now prepared for gluing. We rough it with the shoemaker's knife up to the marked area. The Mexican loop is covered with contact adhesive at the roughed area and the same is done at the marked area on the sheath body. After the contact adhesive has set, both construction parts are pressed together and glued.

The loop is adjusted to the sheath and the end of the loop is transferred onto the sheath with a pencil.

1.3 Preparing the Parts for Construction

With the shoemaker's knife we rough the sheath's backside in the area to be glued.

The construction parts are covered with contact adhesive and pressed together after setting.

1.4 Sewing the Sheath

To sew the sheath, we first mark the distance between seam holes at the already prepared seam groove with the caliper. We chose a distance between seam holes of about 5/16" (eight millimeters), which is now transferred onto the leather stitch by stitch. If the distances do not work out, even towards the end you can shorten the distance by a few tenths and cheat a bit.

> ### HELP WITH PIERCING
> Piercing seam holes into thick leather is usually very strenuous work and needs a lot of force. Here a column-type drilling machine is helpful. By means of the integrated leverage of the feed you can save a lot of force. For this prepare a wooden board that you polish finely on its top and whose edges you round off.
>
> Drill a hole into the center of the wooden board corresponding to the width of your scratch awl. It should not be wider by more than 1/16" (a millimeter) because otherwise you will create ugly impressions on the backside of your sheath.
>
> Fix the wooden board to the extension arm with a c-clamp in such a way that the scratch awl, which is chucked into the tap holder, is going straight down into the board's center hole when pressing downward.
>
> Caution: the drilling machine is used as a press and is not supposed to be switched on during work. To stay safe pull the power plug and make sure the drilling machine is not powered.
>
> If the angle of the extension arm can be adjusted, align it to 0° for the scratch awl to be exactly 90° to the supporting board. Now you can start and pierce hole after hole. During this, the position of the scratch awl can be continuously adjusted to the course of the seam by turning the tap holder.

1.4 Sewing the Sheath

For sewing, we mark the distance between stitches with the wing dividers. We chose a distance of about 5/16" (eight millimeters) for this.

To pierce uniformly and vertically through the thick leather, a column-type drilling machine can be used with the scratch awl clamped into the tap holder. However, the awl is not used for drilling but only pressed into the leather.

The seam holes on the sheath's backside are embedded with the V gouge.

THREADING THE NEEDLE

To prevent the needle from slipping off the thread a special technique is used to thread the needle. For this, the yarn used for sewing is first cut to size. To figure out the required length you can use the following formula:

((Length of seam + material strength) x (number of stitches + extra stitches for the beginning and end of sewing) + needle length x 2) x 2 + 15% reserve

If this formula is too complicated for your taste you can also use an old rule of thumb and take about eight to ten times as much yarn as the length of the distance to be sewn, meaning for a 7⅞" (20 cm) seam you need almost 6' 6⁷⁄₁₀" (two meters) of yarn; for thicker material (more than ½" [12 mm] thick) you need even more.

First the thread is pierced with the harness needle (see below).

With the second stitch you pierce the thread about ⅜" to 1³⁄₁₆" (one to two centimeters) apart from the first piercing. In doing so, you have to take care that the tip of the needle points in the direction of the long end of the thread.

The end of the yarn is then threaded through the eye. For this it has to be twisted slightly so the strands will not come apart during threading. In case of difficulties you can use a threading aid.

Now the end of the thread is pulled towards the eye until it stops at the first piercing. The long end is also pulled over the eye, thus fixing the harness needle. The whole procedure is repeated at the other end for the second needle and we are ready for sewing.

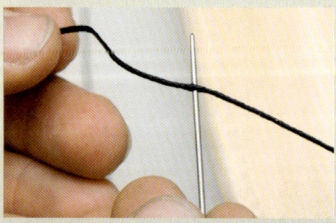

First the thread is pierced with the harness needle; 1 ⁹⁄₁₆" to 2 ³⁄₈" (four to six centimeters) of the yarn is left over at the end.

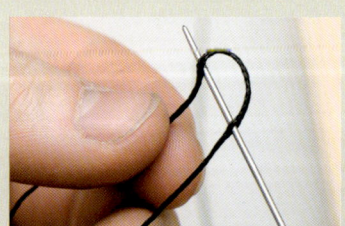

The end of the yarn is now threaded through the eye. For this, the yarn is twisted so the strands will not come apart during threading.

1.4 Sewing the Sheath

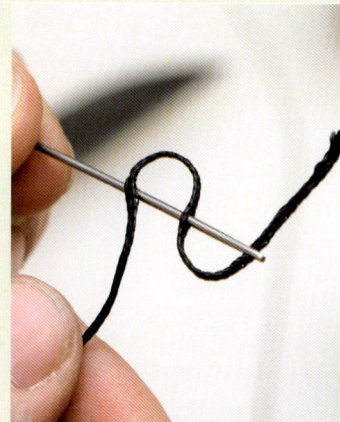

With the second stitch the yarn is pierced about ⅜" to 1³⁄₁₆" (one to two centimeters) away from the first stitch. The needle tip points in the direction of the long end of the yarn.

The short end of the yarn is pulled through the eye until it is stopped at the pierced spot.

The long end of the yarn is also pulled over the eye so the yarn becomes firmly connected to the harness needle.

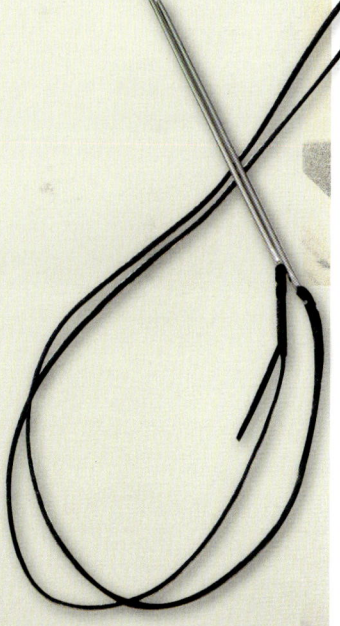

The same is repeated for the other end of the yarn, and then we are ready for sewing.

Project 1: Mexican Loop Sheath

If all seam holes are pierced the seam is embedded on the backside by connecting all the holes with the V gouge and cutting a groove in which the seam will be protected against abrasive wear later on.

We sew the sheath with plastic sinew and a classic saddle stitch. Because the sheath is very large and is difficult to sew in one piece we divide the seam: first we sew together the left side, then the right side. We start sewing at the second hole on the left, upper side of the sheath. The first needle is threaded through the hole and the plastic sinew is pulled through. To have the same length of plastic sinew for both needles we put both needles together and pull the sinew.

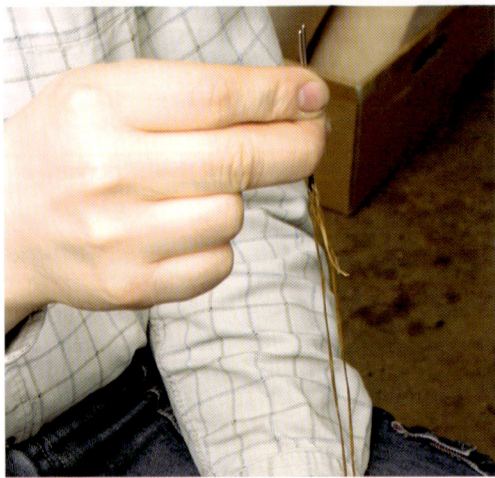

We pierce the first needle through the second hole and pull the plastic sinew through.

Both needles are put together and the plastic sinew is pulled to about the same length.

1.4 Sewing the Sheath

We push the second needle through the topmost hole and pull the thread through. With the first needle we push through the first hole from behind and pull the plastic sinew through. With the first needle in the right hand and the second needle in the left we pull the plastic sinew tight evenly. The sinew ought to be tight but not cut through the leather; optimally, the seam should be slightly pulled into the leather.

Tip: If you have soft hands leather gloves are recommended for sewing. This way you avoid the yarn cutting into your fingers and the ball of your thumb while pulling the seam tight.

Now we push the second needle from the front through the first hole and pull the plastic sinew through.

The first needle is pushed through the first hole from the backside and here, too, the plastic sinew is pulled through.

With even force the plastic sinew is pulled tight.

Project 1: Mexican Loop Sheath

The upper seam is sewn double to strengthen the seam in the upper part of the sheath where it has to endure the most stress. With the second needle we push from the front side into the second hole and pull the sinew through. From the backside of the second hole we push through with the first needle. Both ends of the plastic sinew are again pulled tight. We continue the seam stitch after stitch down to the sheath's tip.

We pull the first needle through the second hole. This way we achieve a double seam for strengthening.

The second needle is pierced through the second hole coming from behind and both ends of the plastic sinew are pulled tight evenly.

1.4 Sewing the Sheath

When we arrive at the sheath's tip we make another stitch from the front side into the first hole on the right side of the sheath and pull the plastic sinew through. Now both ends of the sinew are located on the backside of the sheath.

The right side of the sheath is sewn stitch after stitch as we did on the left side. When we arrive at the sheath tip, we make the last stitch on the left side and pull the plastic sinew through. Now all ends of the plastic sinew from both seams poke out on the backside of the sheath. They are pulled tight evenly and then cut off with the shoemaker's knife, leaving a surplus of about ⅛" to 3/16" (three to five millimeters). Plastic sinew—as its name implies—is made from plastics and can be easily melted and welded with a cigarette lighter. This way the seam is permanently protected from becoming undone.

After continuing the series of stitches down to the tip we set another stitch from the front side of the sheath.

Now both ends of the plastic sinew protrude from the sheath's backside.

Project 1: Mexican Loop Sheath

We sew the sheath's opposite side in the same way and set the last stitch from the front.

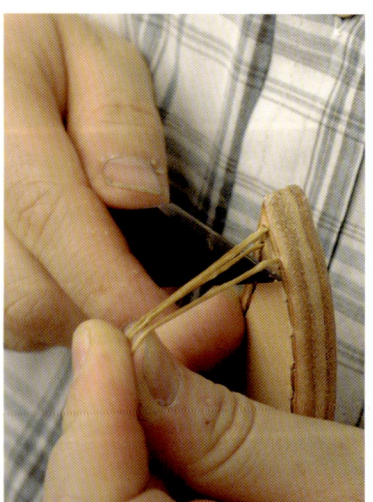

All four ends of the plastic sinew now protrude from the backside of the sheath. They are cut off with the shoemaker's knife, leaving an excess of about 1 3/16" to 2" (3 to 5 millimeters).

Since the plastic sinew is made from plastics the ends can be easily welded with a cigarette lighter. This way the seam is permanently protected against becoming undone.

1.4 Sewing the Sheath

The sewn construction parts are once again fitted together and small irregularities are removed with the shoemaker's knife and edge beveler. Thereafter, the refined areas are moistened, then rounded and smoothed with our horn tool. Slowly our Mexican loop sheath takes shape.

Now the transitions of sheath and loop are cleaned because the leather has been pushed apart slightly by sewing them together.

The cut edges are refined once more.

Project 1: Mexican Loop Sheath

The moistened cut edges are brought to a shine with the horn tool.

The Mexican loop sheath is almost finished.

1.5 Attaching the Protective Strap

To ensure the bowie will rest in the sheath safe and secure later and can't get lost inadvertently we construct a protective strap with a snap fastener. For this, we cut a strap about 1" (25 mm) from smooth, full-grain leather with a thickness of about 2.0–2.5 millimeters, taking the direction of pull into account. One side of the strap we round in a suitable way, using a quarter as a template. When cutting the leather, you have to take care that the edges are cut at a 90° angle.

To prevent losing the knife, we provide the sheath with a protective strap. For this we cut a leather strip about 1" (25 mm) wide from smooth, full-grain leather with a thickness of about 2.0–2.5 mm.

One side of the strap is rounded. You can use a coin (1 5/16" [23.25 mm] diameter) as a template for this.

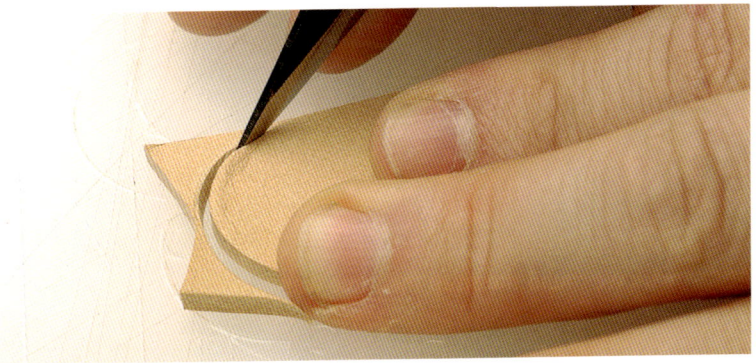

The curve is cut out with the shoemaker's knife.

Project 1: Mexican Loop Sheath

The rear part of the Bowie's handle tapers. Here we will place the protective strap, preventing the knife from slipping out of the sheath. The strap is put around the handle with the ends overlapping. We mark the strap and provide an add-on of about 1³⁄₁₆" (three centimeters). These are needed to set the snap fastener later on.

At the marked place we round the strap with the same radius we used on the opposite side. With the adjustable groover set to a distance of about ³⁄₁₆" (four millimeters), we cut a decorative groove into the leather's top surface. The top and bottom sides of the strap are processed with the edge beveler size 3. After moistening with the sponge all cut edges are rounded with the burnishing wheel and brought to a shine.

We put the strap around the knife handle at about the height of its later position and mark the length of the strap. Because we will later set a snap fastener for securing it, the strap should overlap by about 1³⁄₁₆" (three centimeters).

At the mark we round the strap the same way as on the opposite side.

1.5 Attaching the Protective Strap

We cut a groove about 3/16" (four millimeters) to the outer edges

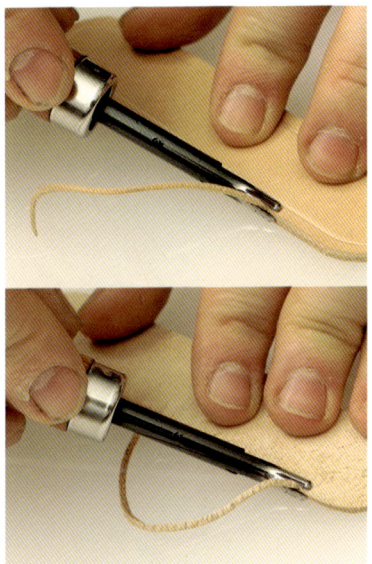

The cut edges are broken on both sides with the edge beveler size 3.

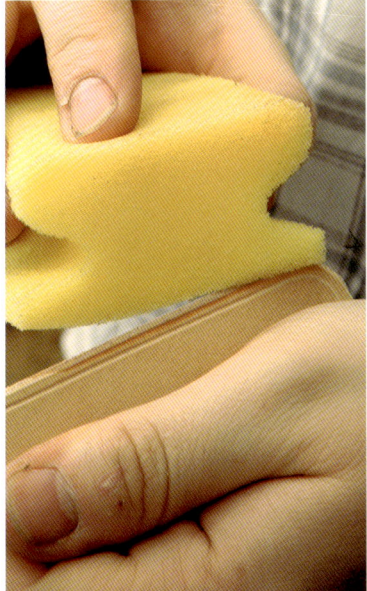

With the sponge we evenly moisten the cut edges.

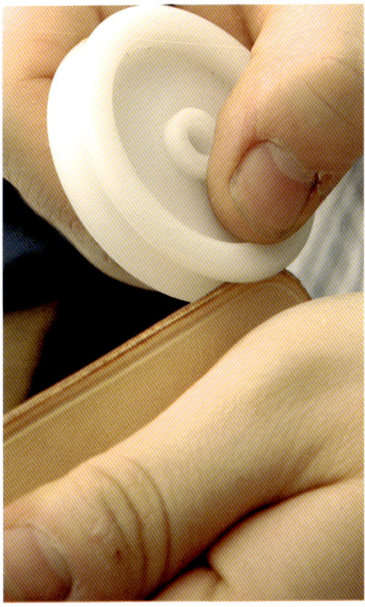

The edges are smoothed with the burnishing wheel and brought to a shine.

Project 1: Mexican Loop Sheath

We mark the center of the curve at one side of the strap, punch a hole with the ³⁄₁₆" (4 millimeter) drive punch, and put the lower part of the snap fastener onto the leather surface. To prevent the snap fastener's rivet scratching the knife's wooden handle we cover it with a small piece of thin kid leather.

The prepared strap is again put around the knife handle with the snap fastener centered on the handle. We unfold the strap while pressing it firmly against the loop and holding it tight. Now we mark the center of the handle on the opened strap.

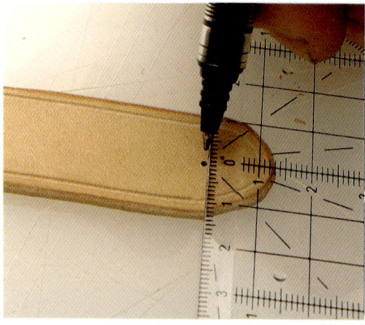

We mark the center at one end of the strap and set the bottom part of the snap fastener.

After setting the snap fastener its flat backside is pasted up with fine kid leather to prevent it leaving dents on the knife handle.

The strap is brought into position and the point is marked where the strap will be attached to the Mexican loop with a rivet.

1.5 Attaching the Protective Strap

We punch the hole for the connecting rivet with the ³⁄₁₆" (4 millimeter) drive punch. The strap is once again adjusted to the handle, folded open, and pressed against the Mexican loop. It should not move because we now transfer the center of the hole onto the loop. At the marked place we punch a ³⁄₁₆" (4 millimeter) hole.

The strap is put into position again and the hole is transferred onto the Mexican loop.

The hole for the rivet is punched through the protective strap using a ³⁄₁₆" (4 millimeter) drive punch.

The hole for the rivet is also punched with a ³⁄₁₆" (4 millimeter) drive punch on the loop.

Project 1: Mexican Loop Sheath

The bottom part of the rivet is put in place from the backside of the Mexican loop. On top we put the protective strap and press the top part of the rivet against the bottom part. Our construction part is put onto a firm steel base and we clench the rivet with the shoemaker's hammer using uniform punches.

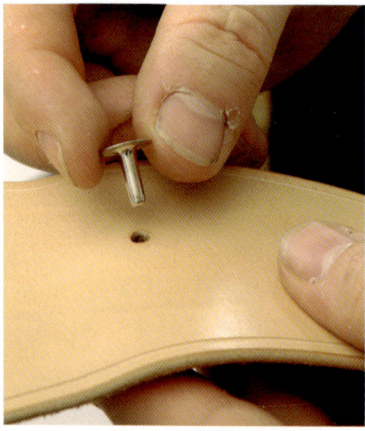

We put the bottom part of the rivet through the prepared hole from the backside of the Mexican loop.

The strap is threaded on from the front side of the loop and the top part of the rivet is tucked on.

The work piece is riveted on a steel base with the shoemaker's hammer and gentle strokes until a secure bond of the rivet is created.

1.5 Attaching the Protective Strap

We put the Bowie back into the sheath and place the protective strap around the handle. Now the center of the snap fastener's bottom is drawn onto the top side of the strap's end lying above. The marked place is punched out with the 3/16" (4 millimeter) drive punch and the snap fastener's top part is pressed into the hole. The snap fastener now sits tight and closes reliably.

To fit the brass snap fastener to the knife we polish it a bit. For this, we cut a small hole into a piece of kitchen wrap and pull this over the rivet head to protect the leather while polishing at the polishing wheel and preventing it from becoming stained with polishing paste. After polishing we clean the snap fastener and remove the foil.

We put the knife into the sheath and draw the position for the upper part of the snap fastener.

We punch the hole with the 3/16" (4 millimeter) drive punch.

Project 1: Mexican Loop Sheath

The upper part of the snap fastener is pressed in. Placement as well as function are checked.

The strap fits: the snap fastener secures the knife reliably against inadvertently slipping out.

Because the cap of our snap fastener is brass with a matt finish, but the fittings of our knife are polished, we do some retouching work. For this we cover the leather with plastic wrap.

At the polishing wheel we bring the brass to a shine.

1.6 Dyeing the Sheath

Before we start to dye the sheath we prepare our workplace. The workbench is covered with paper. Leather dye and a brush, sponge, disposable gloves, and kitchen wrap are put at the ready. For the sheath we chose two colors: as a basic color we use tan—a bright brown with a slight orange tinge—that we combine with brown antique finish. This will provide an interesting color effect later, because the antique finish accumulates in the indentations of the sheath and darkens the color.

The workplace is prepared for dyeing.

We wrap the knife with plastic wrap to prevent it from getting stained.

Project 1: Mexican Loop Sheath

The knife is completely wrapped in plastic wrap to avoid dyeing it inadvertently. Now follows the first step of dyeing, during which we apply the bright leather dye on the sheath uniformly with a brush. During dyeing, the sheath body should not be placed in the loop to easily access all parts. The hard-to-access areas close to the protective strap are also dyed so no bright spots remain on the sheath.

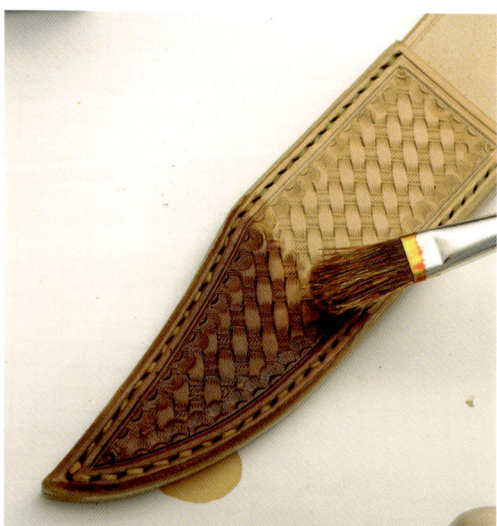

We decided on a rustic, orange-brown hue that matches the knife handle. For this we first dye the sheath with tan-colored leather dye.

Spots that are difficult to reach are also dyed.

1.6 Dyeing the Sheath

After the leather dye has set for a while we apply the brown antique finish. Shake it well prior to application because it contains color pigments. With the sponge we rub the leather finish deeply into the leather and the indentations of the embossing. The rest of the sheath is also covered completely with antique finish.

After a short time drying the surplus color pigments are rubbed off with a sponge and a bit of water. The still-moist sheath is placed into the loop. The knife is put into the sheath and the protective strap is closed. Now the sheath is allowed to dry for a couple of days.

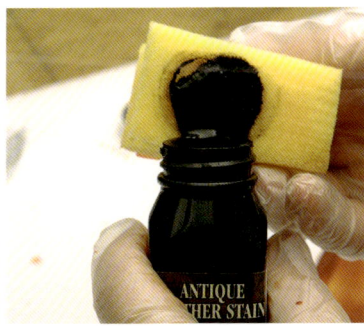

We subsequently shake the brown antique leather finish well and saturate the sponge with it.

The antique finish is vigorously rubbed into the leather so it also attaches to the embossing. Afterward, the excess dye is removed with a sponge.

We push the sheath through the small loop and shape the sheath, which is still wet from dyeing. Now everything is left alone to peacefully dry.

Project 1: Mexican Loop Sheath

1.7 Sealing the Cut Edges and Impregnating the Leather

After the sheath has dried we start sealing the cut edges and impregnating the leather. We spread paper and put our materials and tools ready at hand. We use transparent edge sealant to seal the cut edges. It is applied evenly with a brush on the cut edges, as well as on the visible flesh side of the leather. This prevents the leather from roughening and also provides additional protection. The edge sealant soaks deeply into the leather. It has to be applied several times until a slightly glossy layer is created on the cut edges.

We prepare our workplace for impregnating the sheath.

The flesh side of the loop is covered evenly with transparent edge sealant, preventing the leather from creating "lint" later on.

After the edge sealant has dried the sheath is covered with leather grease. We use a brush to also rub the grease into the indentations of the embossing.

1.7 Sealing the Cut Edges and Impregnating the Leather

After the edge sealant has become touch dry the sheath is impregnated. For this we use a leather grease with high beeswax content. The leather grease soaks deeply into the leather while the beeswax closes the pores on the leather's surface. A shoe brush is best suited for rubbing in leather grease because it allows you to reach the indentations of the embossed patterns. The process of impregnating should be repeated several times because leather can soak in a lot of grease.

After the leather grease has soaked in quite often a bright film of beeswax remains on the leather's surface. Surplus beeswax can be removed with the tip of our horn tool. You can clean the fine embossing with a toothbrush, as well. The strap for attaching the sheath to the thigh—a ⅛" (three millimeter) diameter leather lace—is threaded through the prepared holes at the tip of the Mexican loop and our Mexican loop sheath is finished!

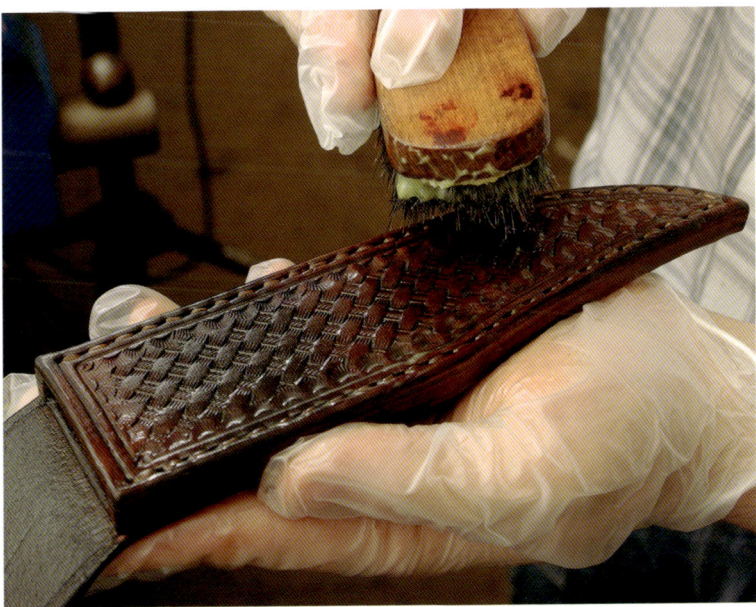

After the leather grease has soaked in we remove surplus beeswax with a piece of cloth and bring the leather surface to a shine.

Project 1: Mexican Loop Sheath

If some beeswax has settled down in the indentations it can be carefully removed with the horn tool.

1.7 Sealing the Cut Edges and Impregnating the Leather

Our finished Mexican loop sheath.

PROJECT II:
Welted Sheath With Snap Fastener

2.1 Planning and Design of the Sheath

For our second project we chose a rather unusual hunting knife. It has a very broad, curved blade with a slightly bent handle. To carry the knife safely and securely, a special sheath construction is needed. We decided on a welted sheath that we will provide with a belt loop, a specially constructed welt, and a flap for securing the knife.

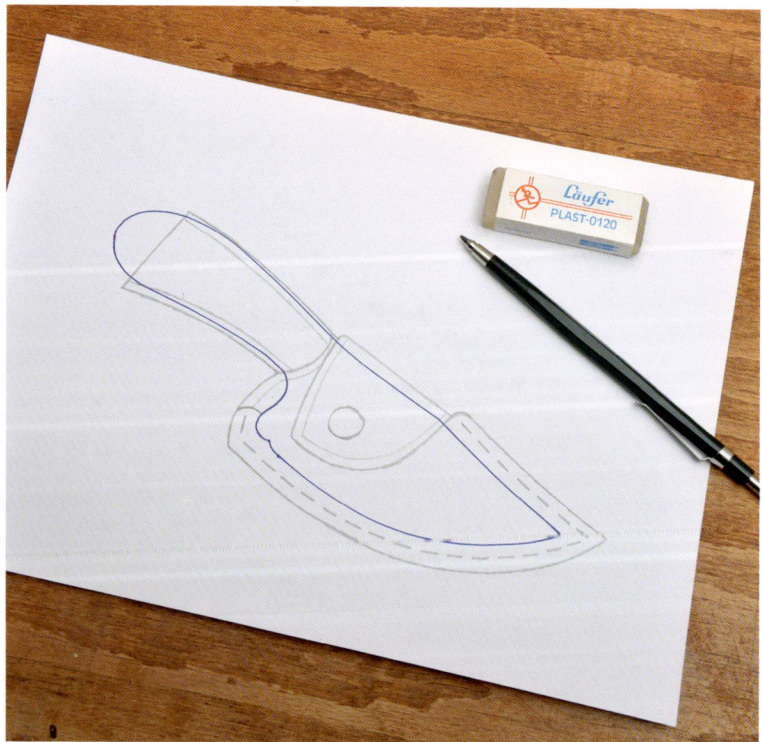

Our second project is less complex than the first one, which is apparent from the design drawing.

2.1 Planning and Design of the Sheath

The sheath itself ought to give a simple and classic impression, so we will not dye the smooth, full-grain leather. It will darken by itself over time and achieve a distinctive patina. We start by designing the sheath and put our ideas down on paper as a sketch.

MATERIALS AND TOOLS

Materials
- 1 scratch awl, width about 3 mm
- thick drawing paper
- 1 handle for scratch awl
- DIN A4/letter size
- 1 base for piercing
- smooth, full-grain leather
- 1 drive punch, 2 mm
- thickness 2.5 – 3.0 mm
- 1 drive punch, 4 mm
- kid leather, thickness 0.2–0.5 mm
- 1 set of shaping dies for snap
- plastic sinew
- fasteners with punching tool
- contact adhesive
- 1 steel base
- 1 set of snap fasteners
- 1 sponge
- beeswax
- 1 cigarette lighter
- plastic wrap
- 1 mallet
  (rawhide, wood or plastics)
- leather grease with beeswax
- 1 shoemaker's hammer
  (with polished steel surfaces)

Tools
- 1 pliers with smooth jaws
- 1 pencil
- 2 pairs of disposable gloves
- 1 eraser
- 1 shoe brush
- 1 geometrical set square or
- 1 piece of cotton cloth
- protractor
- 1 caliper
- 1 paper scissors
- 1 cutting board (plastic or wood)
- 1 shoemaker's knife
- 1 bone folder or selfmade
- horn tool
- 2 harness needles, size 2
- 1 adjustable groover
- 1 edge beveler, size 3
- 1 edge beveler, size 4
- 1 wing divider
- 1 V gouge

Project 2: Welted Sheath with Snap Fastener

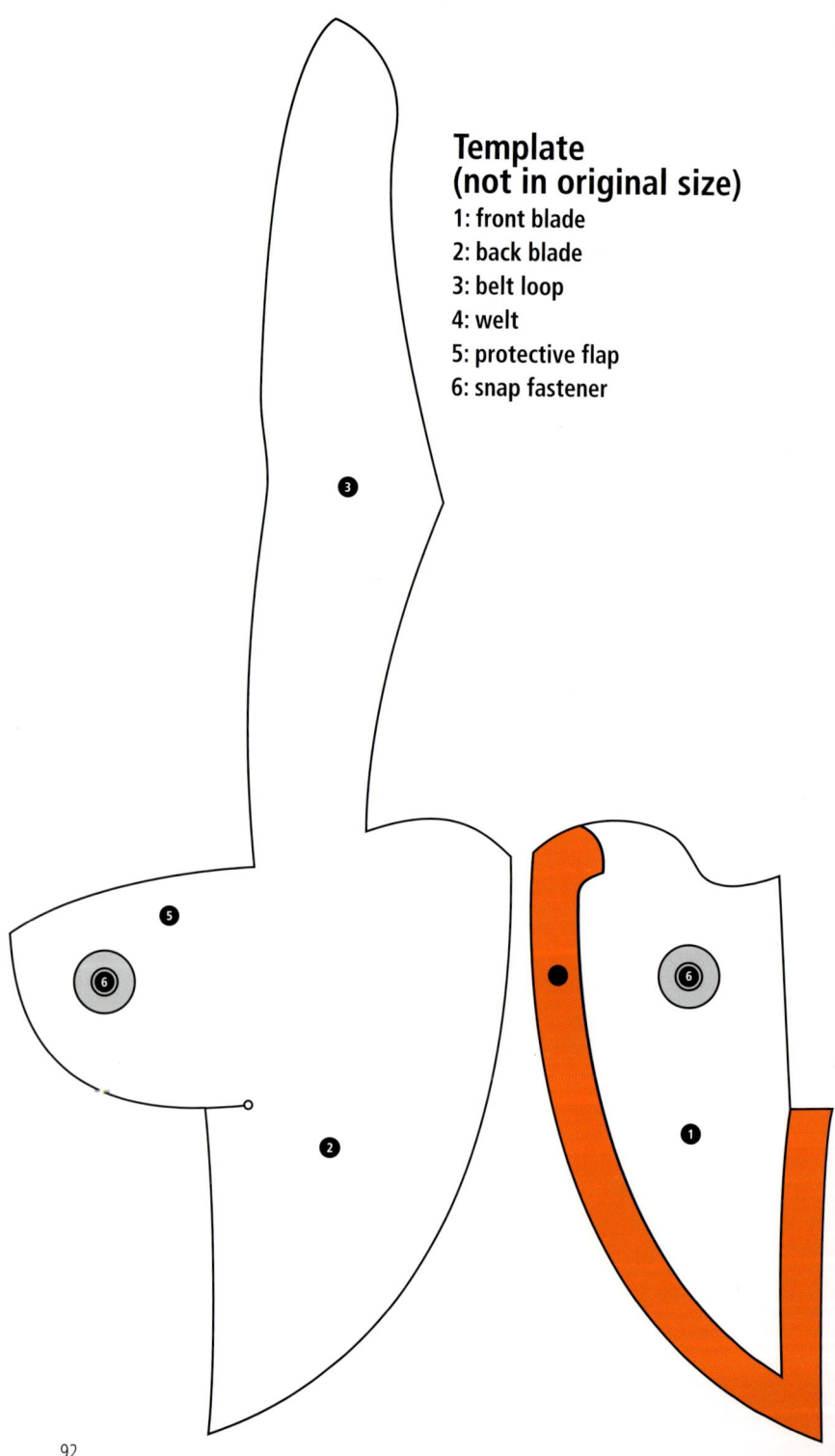

**Template
(not in original size)**
1: front blade
2: back blade
3: belt loop
4: welt
5: protective flap
6: snap fastener

2.2 Creating the Template

At our drawing workplace we start by creating the template. We take thick drawing paper and transfer the outline of the knife with a pencil. To transfer the contour of the handle scales onto the drawing, we use auxiliary lines to mark the beginning and end of the radii. At the knife blade's back—at the place where the blade has a distinct bend—we also set a mark. The protective flap will later reach up to this point.

The outline of the welt is drawn at a distance of about 5/16" (eight millimeters) to the knife blade. At the sheath orifice we also add an extra 5/16" (eight millimeters). Here the welt's nose—which will hold the blade firmly inside the sheath when the protective flap is closed—will be located later on.

The contours of our knife are transferred onto thick drawing paper.

The outline of the welt is drawn at about 5/16" (eight millimeters).

Project 2: Welted Sheath with Snap Fastener

At a 90° angle towards the blade's back we draw two parallel lines at the marked points. Here is where the protective flap will be located. The intended shapes of the flap and the snap fastener are drawn onto the template.

To give the transition towards the sheath orifice a prettier shape, we connect the welt's nose and the space left for the knife's handle with a slight sweep. The belt loop ought to follow the handle contour. Parallel to the auxiliary lines for the protective flap we set the belt loop's end about 1³⁄₁₆" (two centimeters) below the handle's end. The exact contour of the welt's nose is drawn onto the template. It will hold the blade safe and secure inside the sheath. Now we elaborate on the details; the contours of seams and decorative lines are drawn and our design drawing is finished.

The geometrical set square is used to draw the contour of the later protective flap.

2.2 Creating the Template

The contours of the sheath orifice, protective flap, and the snap fastener are drawn in.

The belt loop is sketched following the handle's outline.

Next is the welt's nose, which will prevent the knife from falling out of the sheath.

Seam contours and decorative lines are drawn.

The design drawing of the sheath is finished.

Project 2: Welted Sheath with Snap Fastener

The template is cut out with scissors. The length of the protective flap is adjusted, leaving a surplus of about 1 3/16" to 1 13/16" (two to three centimeters). This way we have enough reserve for later adjustments.

The created template is transferred onto thick drawing paper. To also get a complete template for the belt loop we put the template mirrored against the upper end of the belt loop and draw the belt loop once more. To sew the belt loop on later we add an extra bit of about 1" (two and a half centimeters). We continue the sweep of the belt loop up to the tip. The template for the sheath's back blade is finished.

We cut along the outlines with scissors.

The length of the later flap is checked. Our template should have a surplus of 1 3/16" to 1 3/16" (two to three centimeters).

2.2 Creating the Template

We put the template on thick drawing paper and retrace the outlines.

At the end of the belt loop we turn the template around to draw the belt loop mirrored.

Project 2: Welted Sheath with Snap Fastener

To be able to sew the belt loop on later we add a surplus of 1" (2.5 cm).

The tip of the belt loop is sketched, continuing the contour.

2.2 Creating the Template

We once again take the first template and cut off the protective flap, following the knife blade's back. The belt loop is cut off as well. Now we fit the contour of the sheath orifice to the knife's handle scales. The template is also transferred onto thick drawing paper. Now only the welt is missing, which we cut from our template by following the contours of the knife blade. The welt is transferred onto the drawing paper and subsequently cut out together with the other templates.

The flap of the first template is cut off.

The appendage of the belt loop is removed as well.

Project 2: Welted Sheath with Snap Fastener

We fit the template to the knife handle's contour.

The template is transferred onto thick drawing paper.

With scissors we cut the welt from our first template.

2.2 Creating the Template

The welt's contour is also transferred onto the drawing paper.

Then we cut out all three templates.

Project 2: Welted Sheath with Snap Fastener

2.3 Preparing the Parts for Construction

For our sheath we decided on a version for right-handed persons. If you plan your project for a left-handed sheath you have to draw your parts for the sheath mirrored to our images.

When choosing the leather, you have to take the leather's direction of pull into account. The main stress will later be on the belt loop, which should not expand too much. In our example we used smooth, full-grain leather with a thickness of 2.5 to 3.0 millimeters.

For better visibility, we drew our parts with a black felt pen. Nevertheless, we recommend—especially for an undyed leather sheath—working with a pencil to avoid any kind of stains on the leather.

Before we start to cut out the parts we set a few $\frac{1}{16}$" (two millimeter) holes with the drive punch at the corner points on the sheath's back blade. This way the parts can be more easily cut out with the shoemaker's knife.

The patterns are transferred onto the leather. Our example shows a sheath for right-handed people.

2.3 Preparing the Parts for Construction

At the corner points we punch small connecting holes with a 1/16" (2 millimeter) drive punch.

We cut all the parts to size with the shoemaker's knife.

2.3.1 Making the Sheath's Back Blade

To prepare the sheath's back blade we take the adjustable groover and set it to ³⁄₁₆" (four millimeters). Then we use it to draw a groove on the leather's surface following the belt loop's contour. The tip of the belt loop is skived on a smooth surface to a thickness of about ¹⁄₁₆" (one millimeter) using the shoemaker's knife. This way no annoying steps will be part of the sheath later on.

We start preparing the sheath's back blade by setting the adjustable groover to about ³⁄₁₆" (four millimeters) and draw a groove following the belt loop's contour.

The belt loop's tip is skived down to about ¹⁄₁₆" (one millimeter) with the shoemaker's knife.

2.3 Preparing the Parts for Construction

We fold the belt loop backwards and mark the loop's tip on the back blade's flesh side with a prick of the scratch awl. Now we break the cut edges of the belt loop on the grain and the flesh side with the edge beveler size 3.

The tip of the belt loop and the area it is sewn on later are covered with contact adhesive. After the glue has set we place the belt loop in such a way that the tip is located next to our awl mark. The parts to be glued are pressed together and patted together firmly with the shoemaker's hammer.

The belt loop is folded backwards and the point where the tip is located is marked with the scratch awl.

The cut edges on the inside and outside are broken with the edge beveler size 3.

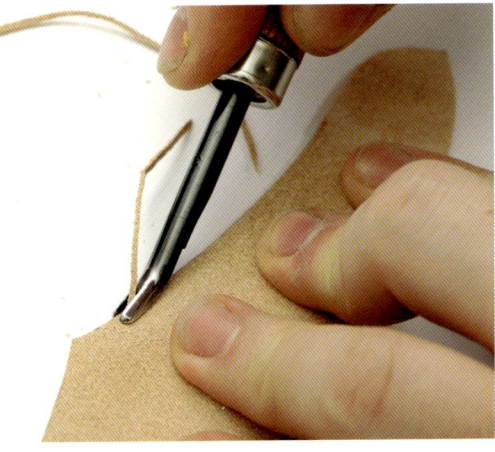

Project 2: Welted Sheath with Snap Fastener

On the flesh side, the belt loop's tip is covered with contact adhesive.

The spot where the tip of the belt loop will be located is covered as well. Then the sheath is put aside for setting.

After setting the belt loop is folded backwards and the tip is adjusted to the mark. Then we pat the bond with the shoemaker's hammer.

2.3 Preparing the Parts for Construction

The upper end of the belt loop is moistened with a sponge and pressed together with the heel of your hand. We mark the upper seam of the belt loop with a pencil and make the groove for embedding the seam using the V gouge. It is important to embed the seam deeply enough so the plastic sinew will not fray during later use while pulling and pushing the knife back and forth.

The upper end of the belt loop is moistened.

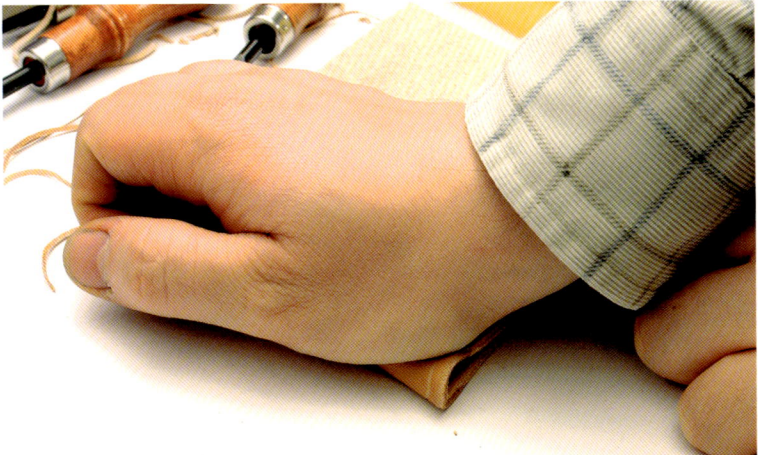

Afterward, we press it flat with the heel of our hand.

Project 2: Welted Sheath with Snap Fastener

The contour of the seam is marked. Please use a pencil for this!

We embed the later seam with the V gouge.

2.3 Preparing the Parts for Construction

The distances between seam holes are marked with a wing divider. We set the distance between holes to about ¼" (six millimeters). The holes are pierced with the scratch awl. For this we use a felt block as a base. During piercing, the scratch awl has to be guided at exactly a 90° angle to the work piece. The awl's blade has to be aligned at a 30° angle towards the seam. The more precisely the seam holes are set the more uniform the seam will be later on.

With the tips of the wing dividers set to about ¼" (six millimeters) we mark the distance between seam holes.

We pierce the seam holes with the scratch awl.

Project 2: Welted Sheath with Snap Fastener

On the sheath's back side we also embed the seam by connecting the seam holes with the V gouge. Embedding protects the seam later on and prevents fraying during use.

Now we can sew on the belt loop. As described for the first project, we use a saddle stitch with two blunt harness needles. We start with the seam facing the belt loop's top surface, sew down to the loop's tip, and then back up to the starting point. When we arrive there, we set another three stitches to strengthen the top seam, as this will have to endure a lot of stress later. We pull the ends of the plastic sinew to the back side of the sheath, cut them off with the ends projecting about ⅛" to ³⁄₁₆" (three to five millimeters), then weld them together with a cigarette lighter.

On the sheath's backside we embed the seam's contour with the V gouge.

The belt loop is sewn on using plastic sinew.

2.3 Preparing the Parts for Construction

2.3.2 Making the Sheath's Front Blade

To prepare the sheath's front blade we set the adjustable groover to a bit more than half of the welt's width, in our case about 3⁄16" (five millimeters). We put the front blade—which we already cut out—at the ready.

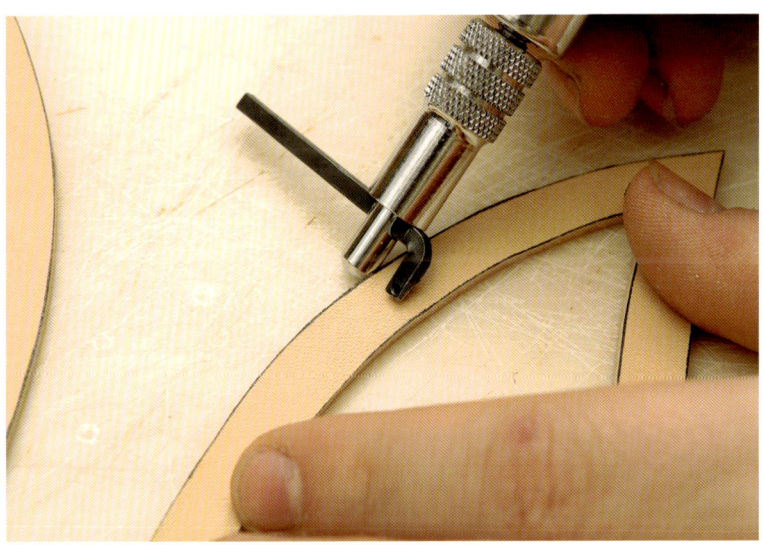

The adjustable groover is set to a bit more than half of the welt's width. Here, this is 3⁄16" (five millimeters).

We cut a groove along the outline of the sheath's front blade.

Here you have to take care that the lines meet at the corner points.

Project 2: Welted Sheath with Snap Fastener

On the leather's grain side we draw a uniform groove with the adjustable groover by following the piece's contour. For this we work from corner point to corner point. The sheath's front blade is turned around and the prepared welt is put on. The welt's inner contour is transferred onto the inside of the leather.

The welt's contour is transferred onto the flesh side of the sheath's front blade.

We mark the spot where the snap fastener ought to be located.

2.3 Preparing the Parts for Construction

Now we turn the front blade onto its front side again and mark the center of the snap fastener. We punch the hole using a forceful blow with the ³⁄₁₆" (4 millimeter) drive punch. For this we use the rawhide mallet and a plastic board as a base.

Into the punched hole we put a hollow rivet that will hold the bottom part of the snap fastener in place. To be able to rivet the snap fastener cleanly by hand we obtained a steel plate for a base. On a soft base quite often the hollow rivet is pressed downwards and forms an ugly "belly."

With the ³⁄₁₆" (4 millimeter) drive punch we punch a hole at the marked spot.

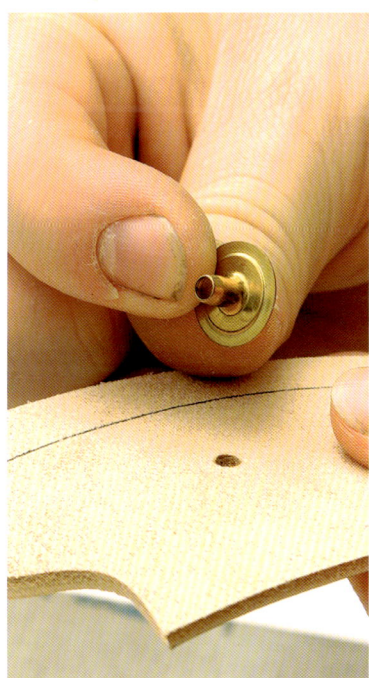

The hollow rivet for the snap fastener is pressed into the hole from the leather's flesh side.

Project 2: Welted Sheath with Snap Fastener

We put the front blade onto the steel base with the flesh side down. We then plug the lower part of the snap fastener onto the hollow rivet protruding from the leather. For easier handling we provided the shaping die with a handle, but you can also use the setting tool that usually comes with the set of snap fasteners or a special lever press.

The shaping die is put on and the hollow rivet is set using soft taps with the rawhide mallet. During this process the rivet rim bends to the outside and creates a ridge that holds the bottom part of the snap fastener in place. Check the backside; it has to be absolutely even so it does not block the knife later on when putting it into the sheath.

The bottom part of the snap fastener is put on.

On a flat steel base, the snap fastener is pressed in by means of a manual punching tool.

The rim of the hollow rivet has been bent to the outside uniformly and thus holds the bottom part of the snap fastener in place.

The backside stayed absolutely flat due to the steel base.

2.3 Preparing the Parts for Construction

We take a thin piece of kid leather and draw the outline of a two-euro coin (1"/25.75 mm diameter) onto the leather. We want the kid leather to cover the backside of the snap fastener to avoid scratches on the knife blade later on. We cut the leather to size with scissors, then cover the backside of the kid leather as well as the marked area on the sheath with contact adhesive. After setting, we glue both parts together and press them together with our fingers. Afterward, the front blade of the sheath is ready for our next work step.

We cut a 1" circle (25.75 mm) from thin kid leather.

The kid leather is covered with contact adhesive on its flesh side.

Project 2: Welted Sheath with Snap Fastener

The previously drawn circle onto which the kid leather ought to be glued is covered with contact adhesive.

After setting the contact adhesive the kid leather is glued on. Now the rivet can't rub against the blade.

2.3 Preparing the Parts for Construction

2.3.3 Fitting the Welt

The cut-out welt is first roughed with the shoemaker's knife on the leather's grain side and created leather residue is blown off. Since we have worked very accurately and the used leather, with a thickness of 2.5 to 3.0 millimeters, is as thick as the knife blade's back, the welt does not have to be adjusted.

We pick up the sheath's backside and cover the marked area where the welt is supposed to be located later with contact adhesive. The same is done on the corresponding side of the welt. Both parts are put aside for setting, then we also cover the marked area on the front side of the sheath blade and put it aside for setting.

The grain side of the welt is roughed uniformly with the shoemaker's knife. This way the contact adhesive can soak deeper into the leather.

The previously marked outline of the welt on the sheath's back blade is covered with contact adhesive.

The corresponding side of the welt is also covered.

117

Project 2: Welted Sheath with Snap Fastener

After setting, we glue the welt onto the inside of the sheath's back blade following the marks. The knife is put inside and the welt is checked with respect to its fit and function. With this construction type, the welt's nose keeps the knife firmly inside the sheath when the flap is closed. To draw the knife, the flap has to be opened and the knife slightly pulled backwards so the nose can release the knife blade and the blade can be pulled out of the sheath upwards.

After setting, the welt is glued to the flesh side of the sheath's back blade.

Now we can check fit and function of the welt and refine if necessary.

2.4 Gluing and Sewing the Sheath

Now the welt that we already glued onto the sheath's backside is covered with contact adhesive and, after setting, glued precisely onto the sheath's front side. The more accurately you worked during cutting the easier it is to put the parts together now.

The fitted welt is covered with contact adhesive.

The outline of the welt on the sheath's front blade is covered and set aside.

Now we put the construction parts together. The more accurately we have worked before the easier the alignment of the parts is now.

Project 2: Welted Sheath with Snap Fastener

The glued construction parts are tapped together with the shoemaker's hammer, which enhances the firmness of the bond. Afterward, the knife is once again put into the sheath. Since the sheath orifice rests closely against the handle scales, we carefully refine the area with the shoemaker's knife until the knife can be put into the sheath without play.

With the shoemaker's hammer we pat the construction parts together. This enhances the firmness of the bond.

The fit of the knife is checked once again.

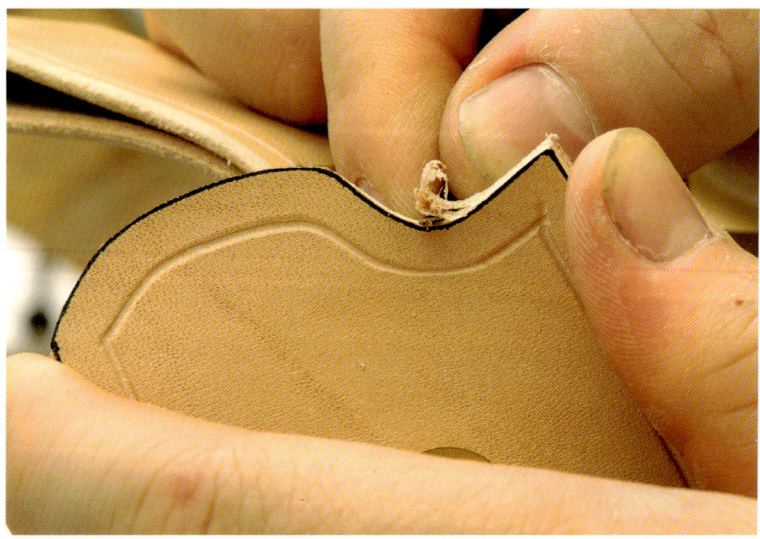

We refine the recess for the knife handle until it fits free of play.

2.4 Gluing and Sewing the Sheath

With the wing dividers we mark the distance between seam holes. As we already did for the belt loop, we use a distance between tips of about ¼" (six millimeters). If this does not work out evenly you can reduce the distance by a few sixteenths of an inch (tenths of a millimeter) to compensate for the difference.

With the wing dividers we mark the distance between seam holes. We set the distance between the tips of the dividers to ¼" (six millimeters).

If the distance between holes does not work out evenly you can cheat a bit and lessen the distance between holes a few sixteenths of an inch.

Project 2: Welted Sheath with Snap Fastener

Now we pierce the seam holes with the scratch awl. As a base we use a felt block, but you can also use cork. The leather is now a bit thicker compared to the belt loop. Check the sharpness of your awl tip; the sharper the edge, the easier you can pierce through the leather. We start in the upper area of the leather sheath and follow the contour of the groove. As we already did while piercing the seam holes of the belt loop, here, too, we have to pay attention to the angle.

This is how a properly sharpened scratch awl looks close up.

The seam holes are pierced with the scratch awl. Here you have to take care that the scratch awl is turned about 30° to the direction of sewing.

The seam's contour is embedded with the V gouge on the backside of the sheath.

2.4 Gluing and Sewing the Sheath

We turn the sheath around and embed the seam by connecting the individual holes with the V gouge. Then we prepare the thread. We use plastic sinew to sew the sheath.

We continue sewing the sheath. Needle and thread are prepared as described in Chapter 1.4. We start with the saddle stitch at the welt's nose. Here we sew the first two stitches double to strengthen the seam. Now we sew stitch after stitch until we reach the sheath's tip, then sew upwards along the sheath's back until we reach the last seam hole. When we have arrived there, we sew two stitches backwards to strengthen the seam. The ends of the plastic sinew now protrude from the second and third holes as seen from the top of the sheath.

We sew the sheath with plastic sinew using the classic saddle stitch. The first seam is sewn double for strengthening.

Project 2: Welted Sheath with Snap Fastener

We pull the ends of the plastic sinew onto the backside of the sheath and cut them off, leaving about ⅛" to 3⁄16" (three to five millimeters), then we weld them together with a cigarette lighter.

Our sheath after we have finished sewing all the seams.

2.5 Cleaning the Cut Edges

The parts of the sewn sheath are ground flush. Afterwards, we break the cut edges with the edge beveler size 4. The inner cut edges are refined with the edge beveler size 3. Areas that are hard to reach are carefully refined using the shoemaker's knife.

With the grinder we grind all the construction parts flush. We start with grit 80 and end with grit 240.

> ### GRINDING WITH THE MACHINE
> You can also use a machine for grinding. Here it is important to use fresh and sharp abrasive paper. The speed of the machine should not be too high, otherwise it may happen quickly that the leather burns during grinding and receives a dark brown or even black crust that can only be removed with difficulty. For large irregularities in thickness grit 80 is well suited for the initial grind. The refinement should be made using grit 240 because too coarse a grinding area can't be polished later on.

Project 2: Welted Sheath with Snap Fastener

We break the edges with the edge beveler size 4.

We refine the corners carefully using the shoemaker's knife.

The inner edges of the sheath are carefully broken with the edge beveler size 3.

2.5 Cleaning the Cut Edges

Since the leather corner at the transition between sheath back to protective flap could be annoying later, we round it with a slight radius. For this we use the shoemaker's knife and cut the corner round without damaging the flap.

We start with cleaning the sheath and de-burr the sheath tip with the shoemaker's knife. With the sponge we moisten the sheath's cut edges and round them using the horn tool. Subsequently, we rub the leather edges until they are shiny.

To avoid getting caught on it later we round the corner at the transition towards the protective flap.

The remaining corners are also gently de-burred.

Project 2: Welted Sheath with Snap Fastener

We moisten the cut edges with a sponge.

They are subsequently rounded with the horn tool and brought to a shine.

2.6 Making the Flap

To shape the flap we moisten it thoroughly with a sponge. To prevent ugly water stains from being created on the sheath later we also slightly moisten the rest of our sheath.

The flap is bent along the sheath's back and onto the front side of the sheath. We first place the upper part of the snap fastener. For this we look sideways between the leather layers and search for the center of the snap fastener with the scratch awl. Both parts of the snap fastener should lie exactly on top of each other and hold the knife blade in place.

To be able to bend and shape the protective flap we moisten it with a sponge. Because our sheath should keep its natural color and water stains may still be visible later, we also moisten the rest of the sheath evenly.

The moist protective flap is folded to the front.

Project 2: Welted Sheath with Snap Fastener

The marked spot is punched out with the 3/16" (4 millimeter) drive punch. The hollow rivet's head is put in from the leather's top side. The created burr is pushed back from the leather's underside using the horn tool.

To avoid damaging the rivet head we need a small cup for setting the snap fastener's top part. This we clamp into the vise between aluminum jaws to have firm support. The upper part of the snap fastener is put onto the hollow rivet and the rivet head is put into the little cup. It is important that the rivet head rests centered inside the cup, because the rim is imprinted in the rivet head in case it slips. Now we rivet both parts together using the setting tool.

With the scratch awl we pierce through the leather at the exact point of the center of the snap fastener's bottom part.

We punch a hole with the 3/16" (4 millimeter) drive punch.

2.6 Making the Flap

The rivet's head is put into the hole from the leather's grain side.

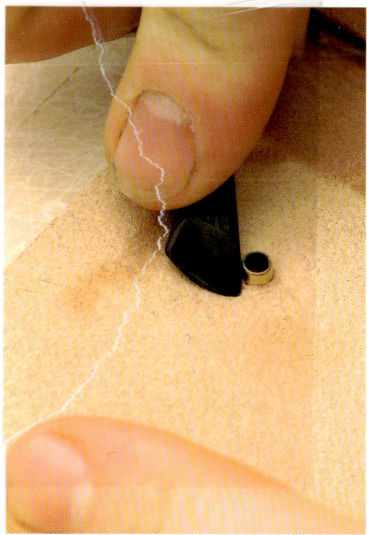

We press back the leather bulge created with the horn tool.

The mold for the rivet head is clamped into the vise.

Project 2: Welted Sheath with Snap Fastener

The rivet head is put onto the shaping die and **the top part of the snap fastener is riveted on using the punching tool.**

The snap fastener is ready for use.

2.6 Making the Flap

We draw the contour of our protective flap onto the front side of the leather. With the shoemaker's knife we cut off the surplus leather. We once again check the shape of the flap. It should not be too large, to avoid catching on it, but it should not be too small either, to make opening easier.

The outline of the protective flap is drawn.

The outline is cut out with the shoemaker's knife.

Project 2: Welted Sheath with Snap Fastener

The flap's shape is checked once more. It can be refined if necessary.

With the adjustable groover set to ³⁄₁₆" (four millimeters) we draw a decorative groove on the top side of the protective flap.

With the adjustable groover we draw a decorative seam at a distance of ³⁄₁₆" (4 millimeters) to the flap's rim. We break the edges on the grain as well as the flesh side with the edge beveler size 3. We moisten the cut edges with a sponge and round them with our horn tool before bringing them to a shine.

2.6 Making the Flap

We break the edges with the edge beveler size 3.

We moisten the cut edges evenly with the sponge and clean them with the horn tool.

Project 2: Welted Sheath with Snap Fastener

To avoid damage to our knife while the wet sheath is drying we wrap it with plastic wrap. The knife is put into the sheath and the protective flap is closed. Now the sheath has to dry for several days until we can continue with the next work step.

To prevent the creation of rust bloom on the knife while the leather sheath is drying we wrap the knife with plastic wrap.

We put the knife into the sheath and close the protective flap. Now the sheath is allowed to dry for a couple of days.

2.7 Sealing the Cut Edges and Impregnating the Leather

Our leather sheath should keep its natural color. Thus, we work with the classic technique. We prepare our workplace and put all necessary materials and tools at the ready. The cut edges are sealed with beeswax applied to the edges with pressure and worked into the leather. By rubbing with our bone folder heat is created, which in turn melts the beeswax and lets it penetrate the leather. All edges and the protective flap and belt loop are treated this way.

The workplace is prepared and all needed materials and tools are put at the ready.

Project 2: Welted Sheath with Snap Fastener

We rub the cut edges with a block of beeswax.

While rubbing the leather with the bone folder heat is created that lets the wax soak into the leather.

2.7 Sealing the Cut Edges and Impregnating the Leather

Thereafter, we impregnate the sheath with leather grease, which penetrates deeply into the leather and darkens a bit. Depending on the leather, this process has to be repeated several times until the leather does not take in any more grease. For the beeswax contained in the grease to also soak into the pores of the leather, the sheath is heated up slightly using a blow dryer until the beeswax starts to melt. Be cautious! The leather itself should not become too hot during this process because it may be damaged. Afterwards, we wipe off surplus wax from the leather surface with a piece of cloth and bring the sheath to a shine.

Leather grease is rubbed into the leather.

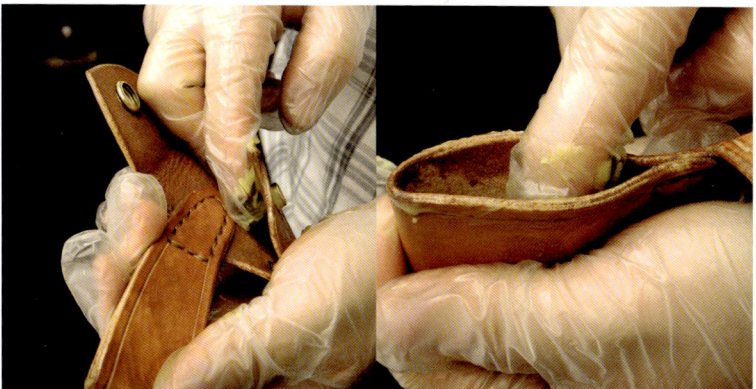

The inside of the sheath is impregnated; leather grease is also applied to the belt loop's inside.

Project 2: Welted Sheath with Snap Fastener

To allow the beeswax to soak deeper into the leather we carefully heat it up with a blow dryer.

The surplus beeswax is rubbed off with a piece of cloth.

2.7 Sealing the Cut Edges and Impregnating the Leather

Our finished leather sheath.

BASICS
Choice of Materials

Since time immemorial leather has been a desired and versatile material. Unique characteristics and surfaces can be achieved using different techniques for tanning and enhancement, depending on demand. Leather can be hard and stiff like sheet metal or soft and smooth like velvet—a unique product of nature.

Which Kind of Leather for Leather Sheaths?

For leather sheaths, all kinds of leather with sufficient stiffness and hardness can be used. Especially recommended is leather that was tanned using plants, because this kind of leather—contrary to chemically tanned leather—does not contain any aggressive ingredients such as chromium oxide that could lead to corrosion. After tanning, leather is divided into several parts. The central part, the back—called "croupon" in professional language—is the best and most expensive piece.

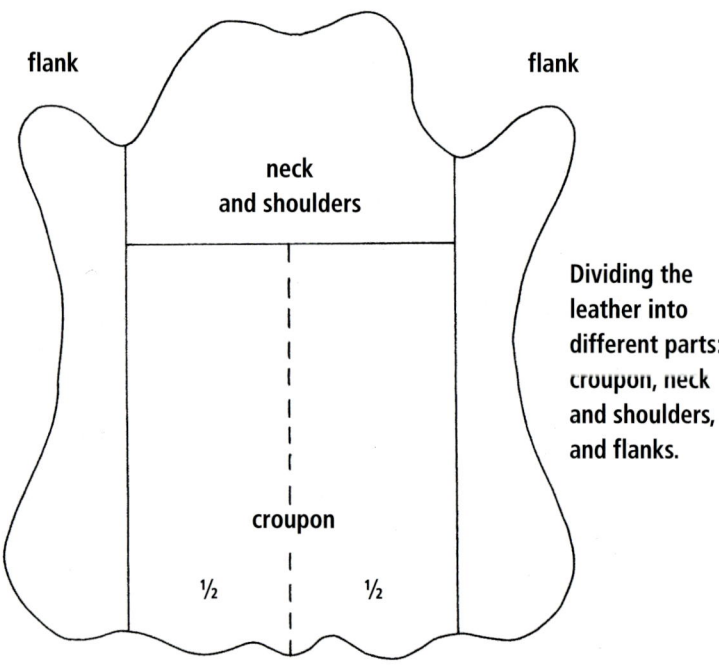

Dividing the leather into different parts: croupon, neck and shoulders, and flanks.

Choice of Materials

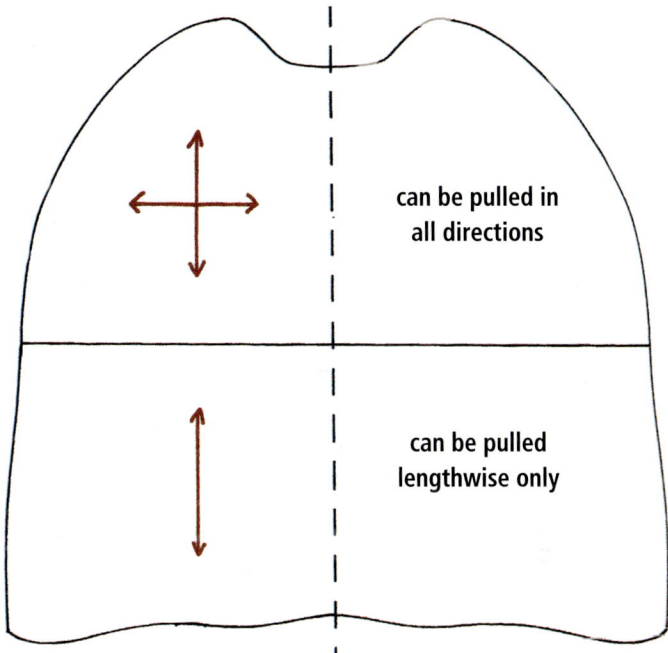

Directions of pull with respect to the neck and shoulders: in the front half, the leather can be pulled in all directions, while the rear half can only be pulled lengthwise.

It is usually cut to size prior to tanning and further divided into halves lengthwise. The croupon is characterized by its extensive and consistent structure. The part containing neck and shoulders is characterized by its versatility. The flanks have a very slack skin structure and are thus used for lining and other parts under no stress or strain.

We prefer using smooth, full-grain leather necks and shoulders tanned using plants, because this material has the optimal characteristics for leather sheaths. Besides that, it is very forgiving with respect to processing and enhancement. It can be obtained with thicknesses from one up to five millimeters.

While cutting to size the direction of pull has to be taken into account. The leather's direction of pull depends on the original skin structure and its quality with respect to strain. In particular, for leather sheaths with belt loops and straps the parts that are subjected to tension have to be cut at a 90° angle to the direction of pull (the direction in which the leather stretches during pulling). Thus, a later wear-out of the straps is avoided.

Basics

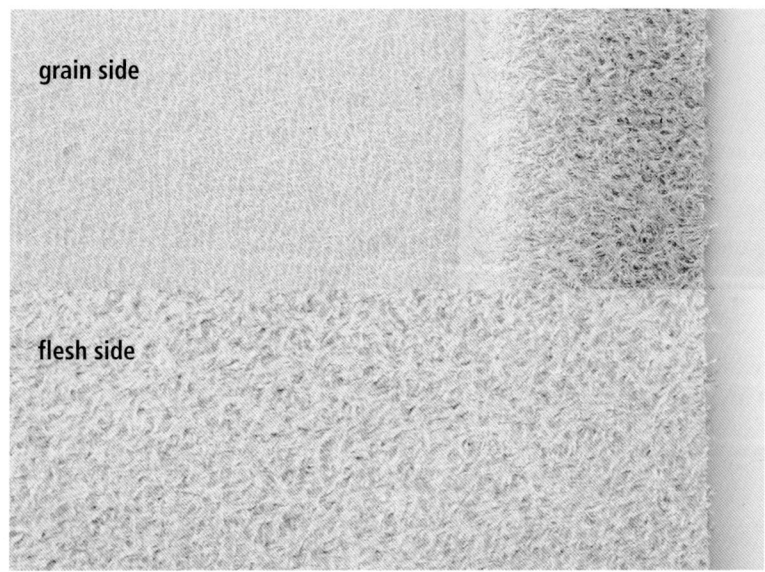

Grain and flesh sides of a polished leather neck with especially dense structure.

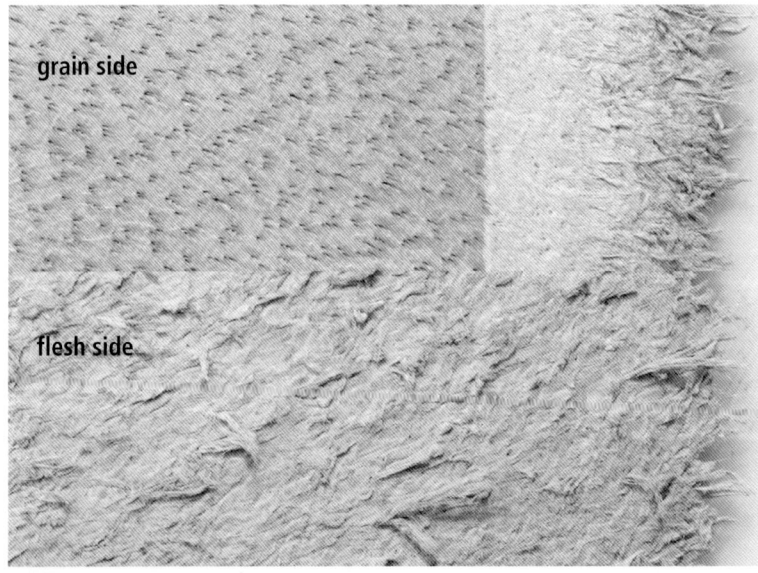

Grain and flesh sides of a polished leather neck with loose structure, not suited for leather sheaths.

The rear half of the neck-and-shoulder section fits the purpose especially well because the direction of pull is lengthwise to the neck. In contrast, on the front part of the neck the leather can be pulled in all directions. The front part is thus especially suited for leather sheaths with separately added belt loops or straps because it can be shaped extremely well.

What to Look for When Buying Leather?

When deciding on the proper kind of leather, special emphasis has to be put on the quality of the leather. High-quality leather makes the job easier and guarantees the piece of leather work fulfills its duty over the course of many long years. While shopping, you ought to look for a dense and tough structure on the flesh side (bottom). By no means should it (the underside) be loose and fringed. Additionally, the grain side (top surface) and flesh side should form a solid unit and not separate from each other.

Which Thread for Sewing?

Different materials are available for sewing leather. Natural yarns such as flax, hemp, and cotton, but also sinews, have been used since ancient times. Modern threads made from plastic fibers have replaced them for the most part because of their better quality. So-called "trout yarn" (for tying flies) is often used because of its high-tensile strength and interesting looks. Trout yarn is a braided yarn made of ten to twenty strands and is offered in different strengths and colors. Plastic sinew made from a multitude of waxed filament yarns is also often used. It has the advantage that the yarn's strength can be adjusted individually by dividing it into halves or doubling it.

Basics

For gluing, dyeing, and impregnation the workplace is covered with paper.

Which Type of Adhesive for Gluing?

For gluing of leather, so-called contact adhesives are especially suited to the job—adhesives that only stick after initial drying and putting the parts together. To use these adhesives, the parts of the leather surface that have to be glued together are first roughed, then the contact adhesive is spread thinly and evenly onto them. After the initial drying, the parts are put on top of each other and are then pressed together with one's fingers or with slight blows with a mallet. If the glue contains solvents, good ventilation of your workplace is absolutely necessary!

Which Leather Dyes for Coloring?

For coloring the leather, leather dyes based on spirit are well suited, but wood stain based on spirit can also be used. Prior to dyeing the leather the color has to be tested on some remnant of the leather. For this, a small piece of the leather used for sheathmaking is cut off and colored with the leather dye. After drying, the test piece is impregnated the same way as planned for the leather sheath. Impregnation usually results in enhancement of the colors and also a slight darkening.

Which Means for Sealing the Cut Edges?
To avoid fringing of the leather around the cut edges a special kind of protection is needed. For this purpose, edge sealant based on shellac, pure shellac, or waxes like beeswax or carnauba wax are suitable. These substances additionally cross-link the leather fibers and improve the resistance of the cut edges to mechanical wear and tear.

The Tools

Preparing the Workplace
A wooden table with a chair and a good lamp will do as a working area. A wooden or plastic board is necessary for cutting the leather and a smooth plastic board or stone surface is used for skiving.

It is important that the surfaces do not have any sharp or pointed corners because these could lead to unwanted scratches on the leather. For gluing, dyeing, and impregnation the working area should be covered with paper. You always ought to clean up meticulously because metal dust and shavings might cause dark stains in the leather that can't be removed.

Cutting Tools

A multitude of different tools are used in leather processing. Some of them can be found in every household, some can be obtained from specialized dealers, and others you can manufacture yourself, if necessary.

Among the cutting tools, the shoemaker's knife is the most well-known. It has a short blade that is about $\frac{1}{16}$" to $\frac{1}{8}$" (two to three millimeters) thick. Most times it is sharpened on both sides, but there are also variants with an edge on the right or left side used only for special tasks.

Basics

Light leather shears (1), rawhide mallet (2), ⅛" (3 mm) drive punch (3), modeling tool (4), space marker (5), adjustable groover (6), edge beveler (7), V gouge (8), handmade modeling tool (9), bone folder (10), scratch awl with handle (11), wing dividers (12), and a shoemaker's knife (13).

The scratch awl is available in different sizes and is chosen depending on the diameter of the thread. It has a diamond-shaped cross-section and is attached to the awl handle. The scratch awl has four sharpened bevels at the tip to cut precisely and without using much force.

Leather shears are strong scissors with fine to coarse teeth to hold the material while cutting.

The edge beveler is a special tool for breaking the edges of the leather. It is available in different sizes and chosen depending on the thickness of the leather and desired radius of the corners.

The V gouge is also used for cutting linoleum. In leather working it is mainly used for embedding seams.

The adjustable groover is used for shaping grooves at a specific distance from the rim of the leather and is usually used for ornamental grooves or for embedding the seams.

All cutting tools ought to be as sharp as possible to cut the leather without creating fringes.

Shaping Tools

The bone folder is one of the most important tools in leatherworking. Quite often it is made from bone, but horn or plastics are also used. Usually the tool has a round and a pointed end to shape the leather. You can also easily construct this tool yourself. A variety of differently rounded bone folders is often helpful.

The modeling tool is also a versatile auxiliary for shaping. It can be obtained in different variations.

For rounding the edges, a handmade tool made of horn or bone is used. At the tip it is fluted using a round file and sandpaper so the edges of the leather can be rounded nicely.

You have to take care that none of the shaping tools has any sharp or pointed corners. The surfaces ought to be polished so you will not inadvertently cut the leather during work.

Other Tools

One of the most important tools is the harness needle. The special thing about it is it does not have a sharp tip, but is rounded. This prevents the thread from being cut when we are sewing back in the opposite direction. The needles are available with different diameters and different lengths and straight or curved.

The space marker is used for marking the distance between stitches of the seam and is available in different variants. Most common is a set with exchangeable wheels and various distances between spikes. The space marker can also be used for ornamental mock seams.

Basics

Drive punches and hollow punches are tools for punching holes or creating small plates. Drive punches are made from round stock and they have a milled ejection opening at one side. They are manufactured with hole diameters from 1/16" to 3/8" (1.0 to 10.0 mm) and are especially suited for punching small holes. Hollow punches and wad punches are generally drop-forged and are recognizable by their "ears" which frame the ejection openings on two opposite sides. They are available from a diameter of 3/16" (five millimeters) upwards. The larger diameters are mainly used for punching small plates. There are also special shapes available, such as ones with oval openings or partly open ones for punching certain construction parts.

GLOSSARY

back blade: the part of the cut leather covering the blade's backside

cleaning out: removing uneven parts and fringes

embossing: decorating the leather using tooling stamps

flesh side: bottom surface of the leather

front blade: the part of the cut leather covering the blade's frontside

grain side: top surface of the leather

sheath blade: the part of the cut leather that will cover the knife blade

skiving: partial thinning of the leather towards the cut edges

twining: twisting filaments into thread

welt: inlaid part that prevents the knife edge from cutting through the seams

OTHER SCHIFFER BOOKS BY THE AUTHOR

Making Leather Knife Sheaths Vol. I
ISBN: 978-0-7643-4015-4

Making Leather Knife Sheaths Vol. II
ISBN: 978-0-7643-4934-8

OTHER SCHIFFER BOOKS ON RELATED SUBJECTS

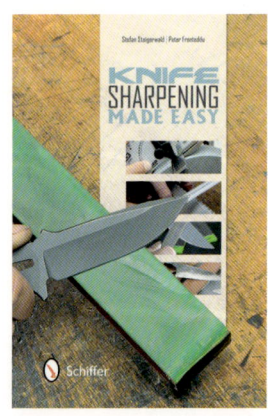

Knife Sharpening Made Easy
ISBN: 978-0-7643-4306-3

For our complete selection of fine books on this and related subjects, please visit our website at www.schifferbooks.com. You may also write for a free catalog.

Schiffer Publishing's titles are available at special discounts for bulk purchases for sales promotions or premiums. Special editions, including personalized covers, corporate imprints, and excerpts, can be created in large quantities for special needs. For more information, contact the publisher.

We are always looking for people to write books on new and related subjects. If you have an idea for a book, please contact us at proposals@schifferbooks.com.

The adjustable groover is used for shaping grooves at a specific distance from the rim of the leather and is usually used for ornamental grooves or for embedding the seams.

All cutting tools ought to be as sharp as possible to cut the leather without creating fringes.

Shaping Tools

The bone folder is one of the most important tools in leatherworking. Quite often it is made from bone, but horn or plastics are also used. Usually the tool has a round and a pointed end to shape the leather. You can also easily construct this tool yourself. A variety of differently rounded bone folders is often helpful.

The modeling tool is also a versatile auxiliary for shaping. It can be obtained in different variations.

For rounding the edges, a handmade tool made of horn or bone is used. At the tip it is fluted using a round file and sandpaper so the edges of the leather can be rounded nicely.

You have to take care that none of the shaping tools has any sharp or pointed corners. The surfaces ought to be polished so you will not inadvertently cut the leather during work.

Other Tools

One of the most important tools is the harness needle. The special thing about it is it does not have a sharp tip, but is rounded. This prevents the thread from being cut when we are sewing back in the opposite direction. The needles are available with different diameters and different lengths and straight or curved.

The space marker is used for marking the distance between stitches of the seam and is available in different variants. Most common is a set with exchangeable wheels and various distances between spikes. The space marker can also be used for ornamental mock seams.

Basics

Drive punches and hollow punches are tools for punching holes or creating small plates. Drive punches are made from round stock and they have a milled ejection opening at one side. They are manufactured with hole diameters from $\frac{1}{16}$" to $\frac{3}{8}$" (1.0 to 10.0 mm) and are especially suited for punching small holes. Hollow punches and wad punches are generally drop-forged and are recognizable by their "ears" which frame the ejection openings on two opposite sides. They are available from a diameter of $\frac{3}{16}$" (five millimeters) upwards. The larger diameters are mainly used for punching small plates. There are also special shapes available, such as ones with oval openings or partly open ones for punching certain construction parts.

GLOSSARY

back blade: the part of the cut leather covering the blade's backside

cleaning out: removing uneven parts and fringes

embossing: decorating the leather using tooling stamps

flesh side: bottom surface of the leather

front blade: the part of the cut leather covering the blade's frontside

grain side: top surface of the leather

sheath blade: the part of the cut leather that will cover the knife blade

skiving: partial thinning of the leather towards the cut edges

twining: twisting filaments into thread

welt: inlaid part that prevents the knife edge from cutting through the seams

OTHER SCHIFFER BOOKS BY THE AUTHOR

Making Leather Knife Sheaths Vol. I
ISBN: 978-0-7643-4015-4

Making Leather Knife Sheaths Vol. II
ISBN: 978-0-7643-4934-8

OTHER SCHIFFER BOOKS ON RELATED SUBJECTS

Knife Sharpening Made Easy
ISBN: 978-0-7643-4306-3

For our complete selection of fine books on this and related subjects, please visit our website at www.schifferbooks.com. You may also write for a free catalog.

Schiffer Publishing's titles are available at special discounts for bulk purchases for sales promotions or premiums. Special editions, including personalized covers, corporate imprints, and excerpts, can be created in large quantities for special needs. For more information, contact the publisher.

We are always looking for people to write books on new and related subjects. If you have an idea for a book, please contact us at proposals@schifferbooks.com.